Philosophical Devices

Philosophical Devices:

Proofs, Probabilities, Possibilities, and Sets

David Papineau

OXFORD
UNIVERSITY PRESS

OXFORD
UNIVERSITY PRESS

Great Clarendon Street, Oxford, OX2 6DP,
United Kingdom

Oxford University Press is a department of the University of Oxford.
It furthers the University's objective of excellence in research, scholarship,
and education by publishing worldwide. Oxford is a registered trade mark of
Oxford University Press in the UK and in certain other countries

First Edition published in 2012

British Library Cataloguing in Publication Data

Data available

Library of Congress Cataloging in Publication Data

Data available

ISBN 978–0–19–965172–6 (Hbk.)
978–0–19–965173–3 (Pbk.)

Printed in Great Britain by
CPI Group (UK) Ltd, Croydon, CR0 4YY

For my family

CONTENTS

List of Boxes   xiii
Preface   xv
Introduction   xvii

Part I
SETS AND NUMBERS

1 Naive Sets and Russell's Paradox   3
   1.1   Sets   3
   1.2   Membership and the Axiom of Extensionality   4
   1.3   Unions, Intersections, and the Empty Set   5
   1.4   Subsets   6
   1.5   Members versus Subsets   6
   1.6   Power Sets   8
   1.7   The Axiom of Comprehension   9
   1.8   Russell's Set   10
   1.9   Russell's Paradox   11
   1.10 Barbers and Sets   12
   1.11 Alternatives to Naive Set Theory   13
   Further Reading   15
   Exercises   15

2 Infinite Sets   17
   2.1   Some Infinite Sets   17
   2.2   Different Kinds of Numbers   18

2.3 Two Senses of 'More'   20
2.4 Denumerability   22
2.5 More Denumerable Sets   24
2.6 The Non-Denumerability of the Real Numbers   25
2.7 The Abundance of the Real Numbers   27
Further Reading   28
Exercises   28

3 Orders of Infinity   30
3.1 Some Harder Stuff   30
3.2 The Numerical Size of Sets   30
3.3 The Reals and the Power Set of the Natural Numbers   32
3.4 The Continuum Hypothesis   35
3.5 An Infinity of Infinities   36
3.6 The Generalized Continuum Hypothesis   38
Further Reading   40
Exercises   40

Part II

ANALYTICITY, A PRIORICITY, AND NECESSITY

4 Kinds of Truths   45
4.1 Three Distinctions among Truths   45
4.2 Analytic and Synthetic   45
4.3 A Priori and A Posteriori   46
4.4 Synthetic A Prioris   47
4.5 How is Synthetic A Priori Knowledge Possible?   49
4.6 Pure and Applied Geometry   50
Further Reading   56
Exercises   56

5 Possible Worlds   58
5.1 Necessity and Contingency   58
5.2 A Posteriori Necessities   59

5.3	A Priori Contingencies	60
5.4	Possibility and Necessity	61
5.5	Possible Worlds	62
5.6	Necessity and Possibility in terms of Worlds	63
5.7	Constraints on Possible Worlds	64
5.8	Essential Properties	66
5.9	The Nature of Necessity	67
5.10	Different Kinds of Possibility	68
	Further Reading	70
	Exercises	70
6	**Naming and Necessity**	**72**
6.1	Two Readings of Statements of Necessity	72
6.2	Scope Distinctions	73
6.3	Julius and the Inventor of the Zip	74
6.4	Rigid Designators	75
6.5	The Causal Theory of Reference	76
6.6	Rigidity and the Causal Theory	77
6.7	De Dicto and De Re	78
6.8	Necessary and A Priori Again	80
6.9	A Limit to Scepticism about A Posteriori Necessity	81
	Further Reading	85
	Exercises	85

Part III
THE NATURE AND USES OF PROBABILITY

7	**Kinds of Probability**	**89**
7.1	Probabilities of Propositions	89
7.2	Kolmogorov's Axioms	89
7.3	Some Consequences	90
7.4	Joint Probabilities	91
7.5	Subjective and Objective Probabilities	94

7.6 Subjective Probability   95

7.7 Action, Utility, and Subjective Probability   96

7.8 Dutch Books   98

7.9 Objective Probability   99

Further Reading   102

Exercises   102

8 Constraints on Credence   104

8.1 The Principal Principle   104

8.2 Conditional Probability   106

8.3 Updating Degrees of Belief—Conditionalization   107

8.4 Bayes' Theorem   109

8.5 Conditional Probabilities and Conditional Statements   110

8.6 Material Conditionals   111

8.7 Indicative and Subjunctive Conditionals   114

8.8 Rational and Metaphysical Changes   115

Further Reading   117

Exercises   117

9 Correlations and Causes   119

9.1 Probabilistic Independence   119

9.2 Probabilistic Dependence   120

9.3 Correlation   121

9.4 Causation and Correlation   122

9.5 Screening Off   123

9.6 Spurious Correlations   124

9.7 Randomized Experiments   125

9.8 Survey Research   127

9.9 Simpson's Paradox   129

Further Reading   131

Exercises   131

Part IV
LOGICS AND THEORIES

10 Syntax and Semantics   137
   10.1 Validity   137
   10.2 Logic and Metalogic   138
   10.3 Different Kinds of Logic   139
   10.4 Truth-Functional Connectives   139
   10.5 Syntax and Semantics   142
   10.6 Syntactic Consequence   143
   10.7 Semantic Consequence   144
   Further Reading   148
   Exercises   148

11 Soundness and Completeness   149
   11.1 Soundness and Completeness   149
   11.2 Proving Soundness and Completeness   150
   11.3 Reflections on Circularity   151
   11.4 Predicate Logic   153
   11.5 Predicate Syntax   154
   11.6 Predicate Semantics   156
   11.7 Predicate Logic—Soundness and Completeness   157
   11.8 Predicate Logic—Undecidability   157
   11.9 Second-Order Logic   159
   11.10 The Incompleteness of Second-Order Logic   161
   Further Reading   163

12 Theories and Gödel's Theorem   164
   12.1 Theories   164
   12.2 Syntax and Semantics for Theories   165
   12.3 Theoretical Completeness   166

12.4 Completeness for Theories versus Completeness
       for Logics   168
12.5 Gödel's Theorem Stated   169
12.6 A Sketch of Gödel's Proof   170
12.7 The Inescapability of Gödel's Theorem   173
12.8 Meta-Theorizing   174
Further Reading   177

Solutions to Exercises   179

Index   189

LIST OF BOXES

1. The Reality of Sets 5
2. The Size of Power Sets 9
3. Russell's Bombshell 14
4. Use and Mention 18
5. Types and Tokens 19
6. The Reality of Numbers 20
7. √2 is Irrational 21
8. The Real Numbers and the Power Set of the Natural Numbers 33
9. The Power Set Theorem 37
10. An A Priori Demonstration that the Angles of a Triangle add to 180° 51
11. 'Bent' Space 53
12. Euclid's Axioms 55
13. The Reality of Possible Worlds 65
14. The Indiscernibility of Identicals and the Identity of Indiscernibles 84
15. Venn Diagrams 93
16. Linda the Feminist Bank Teller 95
17. Bookmakers and Dutch Books 101
18. The Base Rate Fallacy 113
19. The Logic of Randomized Trials 129
20. Truth Tables 141
21. Inference Rules for Propositional Logic 144

22. An Example of a Syntactic Proof   145
23. An Example of Semantic Consequence   147
24. Peano's Postulates   167
25. A System of Gödel Numbering   173

PREFACE

Over the past four years I have taught much of the material in this book to first-year undergraduates at King's College London. I would like to thank the many students who have helped me to see how to present the material better. I am also grateful to the graduate tutors who assisted on my course and gave me much valuable advice: Stephen Tiley, Michael Campbell, Thomas Raleigh, Marion Godman, and Marcela Herdova.

A number of people have commented on sections of the book, including Helen Beebee, Mark Colyvan, Sophie Louise-Walker, Katy Papineau, Peter Ridley, and Michael Gabbay. Thanks are due to them all, and especially to the last-mentioned, whose guidance has been invaluable in many ways.

The book was greatly improved by detailed comments from three anonymous readers for Oxford University Press.

I would also like to mention Parysa Mostajir for dealing with the pesky illustrations with such efficiency and intelligence.

As always, Oxford University Press has done an excellent job in producing the book. In particular, I would like to thank Peter Momtchiloff for his encouragement and good sense, starting from the point when the book was little more than a series of lecture hand-outs. Once the final manuscript was submitted, Javier Kalhat proved an excellent copy-editor and Nicola Sangster a sensitive proof-reader. Eleanor Collins and Jane Olin-Ammentorp were very helpful in guiding me through the final stages of preparation.

INTRODUCTION

This book is written for people who want to understand contemporary philosophy. My aim is to introduce readers to some of the technical ideas assumed in present-day philosophical writing. Once students of philosophy get past explicitly introductory texts, they find that a certain level of technical sophistication is taken for granted. They will encounter references to denumerability, modal scope distinctions, Bayesian conditionalization, logical completeness, and many similar notions. Yet often there will be nothing in their education designed to explain these ideas to them.

What follows is designed as a remedy. I aim to introduce a range of technical ideas without assuming any prior knowledge. For the most part, existing explanations of these ideas are only to be found in the later chapters of advanced texts on mathematical logic, probability theory, and the like. I think that this is a bad thing. The technical ideas that matter to philosophy can be grasped perfectly well without having to plough through a lot of irrelevant and often boring details.

When I explained the idea of this book to one of my more technical colleagues, he complained 'But you're just picking all the plums!' Exactly. I want readers of this book to enjoy the juicy fruit that are normally available only to specialists.

Some will think that a book like this can only be a bluffers' guide, encouraging its readers to bandy technical terms that they cannot possibly understand. I can only ask such sceptics to read on. I think that I explain everything properly. Of course, I have omitted some issues that would have been worth exploring in a longer book. And I have skated over some points of controversy, failing to mention alternatives to some of my assertions. But I don't think that this matters. The information needed to grasp basic technical ideas doesn't generally require acquaintance with every last detail. (In those cases where I have skipped over matters of controversy, I have used the 'Further Reading' at the end of each chapter to point readers towards alternative views.)

The book contains four sections, each of three chapters. The first section is about sets and numbers, starting with the membership relation and ending with the generalized continuum hypothesis. The second is about analyticity, a prioricity, and necessity. The third is about probability, outlining the difference between objective and subjective probability and exploring aspects of conditionalization and correlation. The fourth deals with metalogic, focusing on the contrast between syntax and semantics, and finishing with a sketch of Gödel's theorem. The Table of Contents above gives more information about the topics covered.

The material in this book started off as a ten-week course for first-year students of philosophy at King's College London. However, it has now rather outgrown this origin. I have added a number of extra topics that became accessible once basic ideas had been explained. Moreover, some of these new topics are likely to be challenging for first-year students. While the book could still in principle be used for a first-year course, it now undoubtedly contains too much for one term. It would need to be a longer course, or some of the material would have to be omitted. (I currently omit Chapter 3 and most of Chapter 11 from my first-year course.) If the whole book were to be covered in a normal-length course, it would work better for more advanced undergraduates or first-year Master's students.

Many philosophy undergraduates do an elementary logic course covering the basic mechanics of propositional and predicate logic.

I have long felt that the time spent on these courses could be better used exploring the kind of material covered in this book. It is very doubtful that elementary logic courses do anything to improve argumentative skills. Nor are they normally any good for introducing metalogical ideas. (Indeed they often concentrate on techniques—like 'semantic tableaux'—which positively obscure the distinction between syntax and semantics.)

Perhaps elementary logic courses do more good than I suppose. In any case, this book is not intended as a replacement for such courses, but as a complement. It would be well suited to students who have already done a standard introductory logic course. Not that I presuppose any prior familiarity with logic. When I started writing the book, I thought I might need to. (My original King's College students did my course after a term's elementary logic.) But interestingly this didn't prove necessary. The skills acquired in introductory logic turned out to be largely inessential to the things I wanted to explain. Some prior acquaintance with logic certainly won't hurt, especially in the final chapters on metalogic, but it is by no means essential.

As the above remarks indicate, this book should be suitable for students doing university courses in philosophy. In line with this, 'Further Reading' and 'Exercises' are given at the ends of chapters. However, I rather hope that my readership will not be restricted to university students. As I have said, nothing in what follows presumes any prior expertise. And in my judgement all the issues I discuss are intrinsically interesting, and often downright fascinating. I would like to think that this book can be read with pleasure and profit by anybody who is curious about the technical infrastructure of contemporary philosophy.

Part I

SETS AND NUMBERS

1

. • • • .

Naive Sets and Russell's Paradox

1.1 Sets

Here is how philosophers and mathematicians think of sets. If you have some things—people, cars, trees, numbers, countries, any sort of things—then there is also a *further* thing, the *set* containing those things.

So, if we start with Margaret Thatcher, Tony Blair, and Albert Einstein, for example, we then have the set containing these three, namely: {Margaret Thatcher, Tony Blair, Albert Einstein}. Or if we start with London, Jane Austen, the number 3, and Iceland, we then have: {London, Jane Austen, 3, Iceland}.

Similarly, if we start with all the cars in London, we have the set {x: x is a car in London}. (Read this as: the set of xs such that x is a car in London.) Or if we start with all the countries in Europe, we then have {x: x is a country in Europe}.

Note how we can specify a set by listing all its members, as in the first two examples above, or by specifying a property that picks out all its members, as in the second two.

In the former examples, we are using the *extensive notation* for a set. We name the set by naming the members in turn inside squiggly brackets. {Margaret Thatcher, Tony Blair, Albert Einstein}. {London, Jane Austen, 3, Iceland}.

In the latter examples we are using the *intensive notation* for a set. We name the set by specifying a feature common to all its members inside squiggly brackets. {x: x is a car in London}. {x: x is a country in Europe}.

Sometimes we can name a set in both ways: {John, Paul, George, Ringo}, {x: x is a Beatle}. Note that these aren't two different sets, just two different ways of naming the same set.

1.2 Membership and the Axiom of Extensionality

We say that a set *contains* its *members*, and the members *belong* to the set. If S is a set and m belongs to it, we write 'm ∈ S'. ∈ is the *membership relation*.

The nature of a set depends on nothing more than its members. If A and B are sets, then they are the same set if and only if they have the same members. More formally we can write:

For any sets A, B: A = B iff[1] (for any x)(x ∈ A iff x ∈ B).

This principle is known as the *axiom of extensionality*. It makes it explicit when two sets are the same—if and only if they have the same members. At the end of the chapter we will meet another axiom—the *axiom of comprehension*—that makes it explicit what sets there are in the first place.

Together these two axioms constitute *naive set theory*.

(An 'axiom' is a basic assumption of a theory. A theory can be viewed as all the statements that follow by logic from its

---

[1] Philosophers and mathematicians use 'iff' as a handy abbreviation for 'if and only if'.

axioms. We shall look at axioms and theories in more detail in Chapter 12.)

1.3 Unions, Intersections, and the Empty Set

The *union* of sets A and B is the set which contains everything that belongs to *either* A *or* B or both. We write A ∪ B.

So {Margaret Thatcher, Tony Blair, Madonna} ∪ {Jane Austen, Tony Blair, Iceland} = {Margaret Thatcher, Tony Blair, Madonna, Jane Austen, Iceland}.

The *intersection* of sets A and B is the set which contains everything that belongs to *both* A *and* B. We write A ∩ B.

So {Margaret Thatcher, Tony Blair, Madonna} ∩ {Jane Austen, Tony Blair, Iceland} = {Tony Blair}.

There is also an *empty set*, a set which exists but has no members. We write {}, or Ø.

1.4 Subsets

If A is a set, then B is a *subset* of A if and only if all the members of B are also members of A. We write B $\subseteq$ A.

So {Margaret Thatcher, Tony Blair} and {Tony Blair, Jane Austen, Iceland} are both subsets of {Margaret Thatcher, Tony Blair, Madonna, Jane Austen, Iceland}.

The 'singleton set' {Margaret Thatcher} is also a subset of this set. This is the set whose only member is Margaret Thatcher. Be careful not to muddle up this singleton subset with Margaret Thatcher herself. Margaret Thatcher is a person, not a set.

Note that every set is a subset of itself. (We specified above that B is a subset of A if all the members of B are also members of A. Well, given any set A, all the members of A are certainly members of A.)

If B is a subset of A other than A itself we say it is a *proper* subset, and write B $\subset$ A.

The empty set is a subset of every set. (This might seem a bit arbitrary. *Is* every member of the empty set also a member of every other set, in line with the above definition of a subset? Since the empty set doesn't have any members, it is not obvious whether this is true. Still, let us agree to understand the definition of a subset in this way. Things work out more neatly if we count the empty set as a subset of every set.)

1.5 Members versus Subsets

As we saw above, being a member is *not* the same as being a subset. Subsets of A are extra *sets*, each of which contain some members of A, and as such are not normally members of A themselves.

Even so, in certain cases a subset of a set *can* also be a member of that set.

This is possible because sets can have other sets as their members. Remember that sets are things in their own right, and that any things can enter into sets. So sets, along with ordinary objects, can be members of other sets.

To illustrate how one set can be a member of another, suppose we start with the people Elvis Presley and John Lennon, plus the sets {Margaret Thatcher, Tony Blair} and {Albert Einstein, Stephen Hawking}. Then there will be another set which has just those things as members, namely:

{Elvis Presley, John Lennon, {Margaret Thatcher, Tony Blair}, {Albert Einstein, Stephen Hawking}}.

Note how this set has both people and sets as members.

We can now see how it is possible for a subset of a set to be a member of that same set. For example, consider this set A:

{Ringo Starr, Paul McCartney, {Margaret Thatcher, Tony Blair}, {Ringo Starr, Paul McCartney}}.

The set {Ringo Starr, Paul McCartney} is a *member* of A—namely, the last-named member. But it is also a subset of A, because both its members are members of the set A—namely, the first two members of A.

Note that {Ringo Starr, Paul McCartney} is not a member of A *because* it is a subset of A. For it to be a subset, all that is required is that its *members* are members of A. It is a further fact that it is itself a member of A.

To drive the point home, consider this set B:

{Ringo Starr, Paul McCartney, {Margaret Thatcher, Tony Blair}}.

Now {Ringo Starr, Paul McCartney} is a subset of B, but *not* a member of B.

1.6 Power Sets

The set {Ann, Bob} has 4 subsets:

∅, {Ann}, {Bob}, {Ann, Bob}.

The set {Ann, Bob, Clio} has 8 subsets:

∅, {Ann}, {Bob}, {Clio}, {Ann, Bob}, {Ann, Clio}, {Bob, Clio}, {Ann, Bob, Clio}.

The set {Ann, Bob, Clio, Dai} has 16 subsets:

∅, {Ann}, {Bob}, {Clio}, {Dai}, {Ann, Bob}, {Ann, Clio}, {Ann, Dai}, {Bob, Clio}, {Bob, Dai}, {Clio, Dai}, {Ann ,Bob , Clio}, {Ann, Bob, Dai}, {Ann, Clio, Dai}, {Bob ,Clio, Dai}, {Ann, Bob, Clio, Dai}.

In general, any set with n members has 2^n subsets.

To see why this should be so, imagine that you place the n members of some set A in a row, and that you then form a subset by going though these n members in turn deciding whether or not to include each in the subset. So you have two choices for the first member—in or out. And for each of these you have two choices for the second member—in or out. And for each of these four pairs of initial choices you have two choices for the third member…

So there are 2^n ways of forming a subset B. For each of the n members of the original set, you have a two-way yes–no option of whether to include it in your subset. (See Box 2.)

The set of all subsets of a set is called its *power* set. So the power set of a set with n members always has 2^n members.

So, as above, the power set of {Ann, Bob, Clio} is the 2^3-membered set {∅, {Ann}, {Bob}, {Clio}, {Ann, Bob}, {Ann, Clio}, {Bob, Clio}, {Ann, Bob, Clio}}.

(Note how none of this would come out so nicely if we didn't count the empty set ∅ as a subset of every set.)

Box 2 The Size of Power Sets

Imagine that $m_1, m_2, \ldots, m_n$ are the n members of our original set A, and that we want to form a subset S of this set. We then have n successive yes–no choices of whether to include these members in S, giving us altogether 2^n ways of forming S.

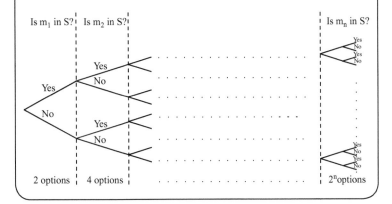

1.7 The Axiom of Comprehension

The 'axiom of extensionality' told us when two sets are the same—they have just the same members.

But how many sets are there in the first place? So far we have been assuming that, for any condition, there will be a set of things satisfying that condition.

The assumption that there exists a set for every condition can be made explicit as the *axiom of comprehension*:

For any condition C, there exists a set A such that (for any x)(x $\in$ A iff x satisfies C).

You might be wondering why I am being so pedantic as to make this assumption explicit. Is it not obvious that there is a set of things satisfying any given condition? For example, if the condition is *being red*, then we have the set {x: x is red}; if the condition is *being a European country*, then we have the set {x: x is a European country}; if the condition is *being Margaret Thatcher or Tony Blair*, then we have the set {Margaret Thatcher, Tony Blair}; and so on. What could be more obvious?

However, far from being obvious, the axiom of comprehension cannot possibly be true. The idea that there is a set for every condition quickly leads to contradiction.

1.8 Russell's Set

Given that sets can themselves be members of sets, there is nothing to stop some sets being members of themselves. The set of *all sets with more than one member* is a member of itself, for instance—for this set will certainly have more than one member, and so it will be a member of itself.

The set of *all things which are not buses, say*, will similarly be a member of itself—since it is a set and therefore not a bus.

Many other sets, of course, will *not* be members of themselves. For example, the set of *all sets with only one member* will not be a member of itself—for this set will have many members and so not belong to itself. Or again, the *set of all buses* will not be a member of itself—for this will be a set and not a bus and so again not belong to itself.

Now consider the condition: *is not a member of itself*.

According to the axiom of comprehension, there must be a set corresponding to this condition, namely, R = {x: x not-$\in$ x}. R will contain precisely those things that are not members of themselves.

However, as Bertrand Russell first showed in 1901, the assumption that R exists generates an inconsistency. For we can prove both that R is a member of itself and that it is not.

1.9 Russell's Paradox

First let us prove that R is a member of itself.

(a) *Assume* R is *not* a member of itself.
(b) But then, since R contains all sets that are *not* members of themselves, it *is* a member of itself.
(c) So we have contradicted our assumption (a).
(d) So 'by reductio ad aburdum' we can conclude that (a) is false and R is a member of itself.

(A proof 'by reductio ad absurdum' is where you conclude that some temporary assumption made for the sake of the argument––here (a)––must be false since its truth would imply a contradiction. 'Reductio ad absurdum' is simply Latin for 'reduction to absurdity'.)

Now we can similarly prove that R is not a member of itself.

(a´) *Assume* R *is* a member of itself.
(b´) But then, since R contains only sets that are not members of themselves, it is *not* a member of itself.
(c´) So we have contradicted our assumption (a´).
(d´) So 'by reductio' we can conclude that (a´) is false and R is *not* a member of itself.

We have now proved both (d) that R is a member of itself and (d´) that R is not a member of itself. Something has gone badly wrong. This is Russell's paradox.

(Just to keep things straight, don't confuse the *final* contradiction *between* the conclusions (d) and (d´) with the *earlier* contradictions encountered *in the course of proving* (d) and (d´). The latter were merely consequences of the temporary assumptions (a) and (a´) respectively, and were used to conclude that (a) and (a´) must be false—since they led to contradiction. But the contradiction between (d) and (d´) isn't a result of some temporary assumption made for the sake of the argument. Rather it is forced on us by the existence of R, which in turn follows from the axiom of comprehension.)

1.10 Barbers and Sets

It will be helpful to compare Russell's paradox with the 'paradox of the barber'.

You tell me that there is a barber who shaves all and only those who do not shave themselves. I wonder whether he shaves himself. And so I reason:

(a) *Assume* he does *not* shave himself.
(b) But then he does shave himself (he shaves all those who do not shave themselves…).
(c) So we have contradicted our assumption (a).
(d) So 'by reductio' we conclude that he *does* shave himself.

And:

(a´) *Assume* he *does* shave himself.
(b´) But then he does not shave himself (he shaves only those who do not shave themselves…).
(c´) So we have contradicted our assumption (a´).
(d´) So 'by reductio' we conclude that he does *not* shave himself.

Your claim about the barber has led to a contradiction. But in this case it is clear enough how to react. The contradiction shows that there can be no such barber. You are full of nonsense. Your claim has been reduced to absurdity. Despite what you say, there can't be a barber who shaves all and only those who do not shave themselves.

Now, at first pass, Russell's paradox calls for the same response. There can't be a set of all things which are not members of themselves, for the assumption that such a set exists leads to a contradiction. But the trouble in this case is that we can't just leave it at that. For the assumption that there is a set of all things which are not members of themselves isn't just some spurious claim made in idle conversation, like your story about the barber. It is an inescapable consequence of what looked like an obvious assumption about sets, namely, the assumption that there is a set corresponding to every condition. If we are to reject the set of all things which are not members of themselves, we have no choice but to give up this axiom of comprehension.

Russell's paradox arises because sets are things and so the axiom of comprehension—there is a set corresponding to every condition on things—also applies to conditions on sets. But the set we get from a condition on sets will depend on what sets are available as candidate members to start with—which is precisely what the axiom of comprehensions was supposed to tell us. What we have seen is that this implicit circularity is not only worrisome but *vicious* in the sense that it generates contradictions.

1.11 Alternatives to Naive Set Theory

It is common to refer to the axioms of extensionality and comprehension as together comprising 'naive set theory'. Certainly these two assumptions seem to capture the intuitive notion of a set. Sets are defined by their members (extensionality) and there is a set for any characterizable plurality of things (comprehension).

But Russell's paradox shows that naive set theory is too naive. In particular, it shows that naive set theory contradicts itself. Some philosophers take this to be further evidence against the reality of sets. But most mathematicians and logicians respond by seeking to replace the intuitive notion of a set by a more sophisticated understanding which is free of inconsistency. This improved understanding must somehow avoid positing a set of all things that are not members of themselves, otherwise inconsistency will inevitably return. So modern set theories all modify the axiom of comprehension in one way or another so as to limit the range of admissible sets. We needn't go into details. From now on I shall simply assume that talk of sets has somehow been made consistent.

Box 3 Russell's Bombshell

In 1902, just as he was putting the finishing touches to the second volume of his *Basic Laws of Arithmetic*, the great German logician Gottlob Frege received a letter from Bertrand Russell about the set of all things that are not members of themselves. In an Appendix to the volume Frege said 'A scientist can hardly meet with anything more undesirable than to have the foundations give way just as the work is finished. I was put in this position by a letter from Mr Bertrand Russell when the work was nearly through the press.' In fact Frege himself never found a satisfactory way of dealing with Russell's paradox. But subsequent mathematicians and logicians, including Russell himself, have developed a number of different ways of avoiding it.

SETS AND NUMBERS

FURTHER READING

Eric Steinhart's *More Precisely: The Math You Need To Do Philosophy* (Broadview Press 2009) is a useful introductory complement to the present book. The first two chapters deal with basic set theory in rather more detail than I have.

Michael Potter's *Set Theory and its Philosophy* (Oxford University Press 2004) is an advanced philosophical introduction to the material covered in the first three chapters of this book.

Mary Tiles' *Philosophy of Set Theory; An Historical Introduction to Cantor's Paradise* (Dover Books 2004) covers much of the same ground.

EXERCISES

1. What is the union of the following pairs of sets?

   (a) {Abe, Bertha}, {Bertha, Carl}
   (b) {2, 5, 7, 11, 13}, {1, 5, 11, 13}
   (c) {x: x is a child aged 7–12}, {x: x is a child aged 10–15}
   (d) {France, Germany, Italy}, {Germany, Italy}
   (e) {France, Germany, Italy}, {India, China}
   (f) {x: x lives in Germany}, {x: x lives in Europe}
   (g) {x: x lives in China}, {x: x lives in Europe}
   (h) {x: x weighs more than 10 kilos}, {x: x weighs more than 7 kilos}

2. What is the intersection of each of the above pairs of sets?

3. List all the subsets of the following sets.

   (a) {Abe, Bertha}
   (b) {7, 8, 9}

4. Give the power sets of the following sets.

   (a) {1, 7}
   (b) {London, Manchester, Birmingham}

5. Consider the set $\{1, 2, 3, 7, 8\}$.

Which of the following items are (a) members, (b) subsets, or (c) neither?

$2, \{7, 8\}, \{2, 3\}, \{\}, 3, \{1, 2, 3, \{7,8\}\}$

6. Consider the set $\{1, 2, 3, \{7, 8\}, \{2, 3\}\}$.

Which of the following items are (a) members, (b) subsets, or (c) neither?

$2, \{7, 8\}, \{2, 3\}, \{\}, 3, \{1, 2, 3, \{7, 8\}\}$

7. (A): 'This sentence is false.'

Show carefully that this statement leads to a contradiction. (Hint: first assume that (A) is true, then assume that it is not true.)

2

Infinite Sets

2.1 Some Infinite Sets

Some sets have infinitely many members.

Think of the set of all the New Year's Eves from here to eternity.

Or if you don't believe in eternity, think of the set of all the spatial points between London and New York. (Since there will always be another point between any two distinct such points, there will be no end of them.)

Again, think of the set of all grammatical English sentences. (Since there is no word limit on the length of English sentences, we can always go on making longer sentences from shorter ones by such devices as adding 'John said that' to the beginning, or putting 'and then they had tea.' at the end.)

These are slightly messy examples. If you want a nice clean example of an infinite set, simply take the set of all the natural numbers, $\{0, 1, 2, 3, \ldots\}$.

While we are on numbers, take care not to confuse numbers with the *numerals* that name them. (See Boxes 4 and 5.) Numerals are *words* like 'one' and 'two' or *symbols* like '1' and '2'. Numbers are the more abstract things that these numerals name. The English word 'two' is a

Philosophers are very fussy (because they often need to be) about distinguishing words from the things that they refer to. If you want to talk about the word rather than the thing, you must put the word in quotes to form a name of that word itself. Here are some examples that illustrate this device.

London contains ten million people, but 'London' contains six letters.
Jack is an unpopular person, but 'Jack' is a popular name.
Seven is an odd number, but 'seven' is an English word—a numeral.
{John, Paul, George, Ringo} is the same set as {x: x is a Beatle}, but '{John, Paul, George, Ringo}' and '{x: x is a Beatle}' are two different names for that set.

On the left-hand side of these examples we *use* the names, on the right we *mention* them.

different word from the French word 'deux', but they both name the same number. Again, the Arabic '2' is a different symbol from the Roman 'II' but they also both name the same number. Numerals are signs used in specific representation systems. Numbers themselves are timeless entities that transcend the perspective of any given system of representation. (See Box 6.)

2.2 Different Kinds of Numbers

The most basic numbers are the *natural numbers*: 0, 1, 2, 3,...

If we add the negative whole numbers to the natural numbers, then we get the *integers*: ...-3, -2, -1, 0, 1, 2, 3...

In addition to the integers, we also want to recognize various kinds of intermediate numbers, numbers that fall between the integers.

The simplest are the *rational numbers,* namely those that can be expressed as fractions of the form p/q, where p and q are integers.

But we also need to recognize further numbers that are not rational.

For example, $\sqrt{2}$ is not rational. There is no way to express $\sqrt{2}$ in the form p/q where p and q are integers. (See Box 7.)

Similarly, π (the ratio of a circle's circumference to its diameter) is not rational. It cannot be expressed as p/q with integral p and q either.

Many other numbers are similarly irrational.

The *real* numbers comprise both the rational and irrational numbers.

Any real number can be represented by an infinitely long decimal expansion: e.g. 23.17564839...

Box 5 Types and Tokens

cat cat

   Question. How many words were there in the previous line? *Answer.* One word *type,* but two *tokens* of that type.

   The term " 'cat' " can refer either to the type word or to some specific token of it.

   Thus: *'cat' occurs often in children's stories.* Here I use " 'cat' " to refer to a word type.

   But now consider: *the first 'cat' at the beginning of this Box could have been written with a capital letter.* Here I use " 'cat' " to refer to a specific token of the relevant type.

   (Note how I have to use double quotes—" 'cat' "—to *mention* the *name* of the original word, that is, the name that we formed by putting that original word in single quotes.)

In this format, we can distinguish the rational numbers from the irrational ones by the fact that the rational numbers will eventually display some recurring sequence of digits. So for example, 1/11 is 0.090909...and 2/7 is 0.285714285714285714...(See the Exercises for some hints about how to show that the rational numbers are just those whose decimal expansions recur.)

2.3 Two Senses of 'More'

Here is a good question. Are there more natural numbers than even numbers?

In one obvious sense the answer must be yes. The set of even numbers {0, 2, 4, 6,...} is a *proper subset* of the set of natural numbers {0, 1, 2, 3, ...}. The latter set contains all the members of the former set and then some. There are plenty of natural numbers that aren't even, but no even numbers that aren't natural.

Box 7 $\sqrt{2}$ is Irrational

....

Suppose (for the sake of a 'reductio ad absurdum' proof) that $\sqrt{2}$ *is* rational and so can be represented as p/q, where p and q are integers, and suppose further that p and q have no common factors, that is, that all cancelling has been done. Then it follows:

$\sqrt{2} = p/q$

$2 = p^2/q^2$

$2q^2 = p^2$

So p must be an even number (since its square is an even number). So, for some integer r, p must be 2r. So

$p^2 = 4r^2$

And, since we already know that $2q^2 = p^2$, it follows that

$q^2 = 2r^2$

So q must be an even number too. But now q and p are both even, which contradicts the supposition that $\sqrt{2}$ is rational and represented as p/q with no common factors. So by reductio we can conclude that $\sqrt{2}$ is irrational.

When the Greeks first discovered that $\sqrt{2}$ is irrational, it freaked them out. They knew from Pythagoras' theorem that $\sqrt{2}$ is the length of the hypotenuse of a right-angled triangle whose other sides are each of length 1. But the irrationality of $\sqrt{2}$ means that there can be no unit of length that will fit exactly q times into these short sides and p times into the hypotenuse (for if there were, then $\sqrt{2}$ would equal p/q). To the Greeks, this seemed to contradict the very idea of length. It is said that the Greek mathematicians who first proved the irrationality of $\sqrt{2}$ tried to keep their discovery a secret.

But in a different sense the answer is no. The even numbers can be *paired up one-to-one* with the naturals. In this sense there are just as many even numbers as natural numbers.

0	2	4	6	8	...
0	1	2	3	4	...

This mapping gives a unique even number for every natural number, and vice versa.

There is no contradiction here. We can distinguish two senses in which set A can contain 'more members' than set B. In the first sense (call it the 'subset' sense), it simply means that B is a proper subset of A. In the second sense (the 'pairing' sense), it means rather that any attempt to pair the members of A one-to-one with those of B will leave some members of A unpaired.

There are more natural numbers than even numbers in the subset sense, but not in the pairing sense—for the pairing illustrated above succeeds in matching every natural number with its own even number.

When we are dealing with finite sets, the two senses of 'more' coincide. If a finite set B is a proper subset of finite set A, then the As can't all be paired up one-to-one with the Bs, for there won't be enough Bs—any attempted pairing will leave some extra As unpaired.

But with infinite sets, B can be a proper subset of A, and still be paired up one-to-one with the As—for now the Bs won't automatically run out before we get to the end of the As.

This is in fact a defining characteristic of infinite sets. The members of any infinite set, but of no finite set, can be paired up one-to-one with the members of some of its proper subsets.

2.4 Denumerability

The odd numbers can also be paired one-to-one with the natural numbers.

		3	5	7	9	...
0				2	3	4	...

So can the squared whole numbers.

0				4	9		6	...
0				2	3	4	...

And all the integers.

0	-		+		-2	+2	...
0				2	3	4	...

What about the rational numbers? At first sight it might seem that there are too many. There really are an awful lot. In particular, given any two rational numbers, however close together, there will always be another rational number in between them. (Mathematicians call this property 'density'.) You might think that this would block any attempt to line them up with the natural numbers.

Surprisingly, however, the rational numbers can also be paired up one-to-one with the natural numbers. To see this, consider the following grid. It clearly contains all the rational numbers. And the arrows indicate a systematic way of going through the grid in sequence and thereby placing the rational numbers in a numerical order.[1]

---

[1] A little complication. If we list the rational numbers as in the diagram below, any given rational number will recur in different guises at different points in the list. For example, we will not only have 1/2, but later on 2/4, 3/6, and so on. Since these are all the same rational number, just written in different ways, our list won't really pair each rational number with a *unique* natural number. The remedy is to complicate the listing procedure a bit—before writing down the nth rational number, check that it hasn't already occurred in the list, and throw it away if it has.

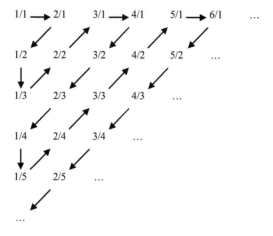

Whenever the members of a set can be paired one-to-one with the natural numbers, we say the set is *denumerable*. A denumerable set is one that can be placed in a numerical list. A numerical list, if you think about it, just *is* a pairing of the listed items with the natural numbers— the first in the list with 1, the second with 2, and so on.

2.5 More Denumerable Sets

Many unruly-looking sets can be shown to be denumerable.

Take the set of all rectangles with rational length and breadth, for example. Each of these is defined by two rational numbers. Given that we can place all the rational numbers themselves in a numerical list, by the grid trick above, we can thus equate each of these pairs of rational numbers with a pair of *natural* numbers. And then we can apply the grid technique once more, to place these pairs of natural numbers themselves in a numerical list. This will then amount to a numerical list of the rectangles we started with.

Or take the set of all English sentences. To place these in a numerical list, consider all finitely long strings of English letters (counting a space as a 27th letter). Now order the one-letter strings alphabetically, then the two-letter strings, and so on. Now go through the resulting list and throw away all the strings which don't make sense as English sentences. You'll be left with a numerical list of English sentences.

There are many similar examples of denumerable sets.

2.6 The Non-Denumerability of the Real Numbers

We have just seen that many complicated-looking infinite sets turn out to be denumerable. Does this hold for all infinite sets? Our surprising success at pairing the rational numbers and other unpromising-looking sets with the natural numbers might make you think that a similar trick can be pulled with all infinite sets. But that would be a mistake. The *real numbers* cannot be paired one-to-one with the natural numbers. They are *non*-denumerable. Indeed the reals between 0 and 1, or in any finite interval, are non-denumerable.

To show this, suppose (for the sake of another reductio argument) that the reals between 0 and 1 *were* denumerable. Then they could be paired up with the natural numbers in some way. To illustrate, suppose the pairing starts as in the list below. (This is just for illustration—the argument will work whatever the pairing.)

1	0.123456…
2	0.234567…
3	0.789012…
4	0.890123…

Now construct a new number according to the following rule: make the first digit one more than the first digit of the first number in this list, the second digit one more than the second digit of the second number, the third digit one more than the third digit of the third number, and so on...(using 0 as 'one more than 9' whenever the nth digit in the nth number is 9).

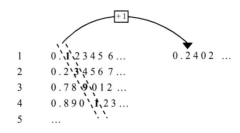

So, given our supposed initial listing of the reals, our new number will be 0.2402...And note that this new number *can't be anywhere in the original list*, since it differs from the first number in the first digit, from the second in the second digit, and so on.[2]

This is Cantor's famous diagonal argument. It shows that there are more real numbers than natural numbers *even in the one-to-one pairing*

---

[2] There is a little complication in this diagonal proof too. Some real numbers have two decimal representations. Consider for example 0.999... = 3 x 0.333... = 3 x 1/3 = 1. This shows that 0.999...and 1...are the same real number written in different ways. And this might make you worry that Cantor's argument only proves that there is a 'diagonal *representation*' that isn't in the original list of decimal *representations*, not that there is a real *number* that isn't among the *numbers* named by that list—for maybe the 'diagonal representation' is just an alternative name for one of the numbers already listed.

Well, it would be interesting enough to know that the set of decimal representations is itself non-denumerable, even if the real numbers themselves aren't. But in any case it is easy enough to tighten the proof so as to plug this hole. One of the Exercises at the end of Chapter 3 covers this.

sense of 'more'. If you try to pair up the reals with the naturals you will always have some real number left over. Given any supposed listing of the reals, it is always possible to construct another real number that isn't in that list.

2.7 The Abundance of the Real Numbers

The reals are very abundant indeed. To get some feel for this, recall that the real numbers are represented by *infinitely* long decimal strings, including strings that display no recurring patterns. The other entities we have been dealing with (rational numbers, sentences, …) can all be represented in finite terms. This doesn't stop there being infinitely many rational numbers or sentences—finite representations can get longer and longer. But once we switch to *infinitely* long strings of digits, we are dealing with a quite different order of plurality.

The example of the reals shows that infinite sets come in different sizes. There is the size shared by all the denumerable sets. But the real numbers are bigger again. In the next chapter we shall explore the way in which different infinite sets can have different sizes in this way.

FURTHER READING

Numbers: A Very Short Introduction by Peter Higgins (Oxford University Press 2011) explains the different kinds of numbers.

The last two chapters of Eric Steinhart's *More Precisely: The Math You Need To Do Philosophy* (Broadview Press 2009) deal with infinite sets and the variety of infinite numbers.

An Introduction to the Philosophy of Mathematics by Mark Colyvan (Cambridge University Press 2012) is a short and punchy introduction to the philosophical issues raised by numbers and mathematical objects.

James Robert Brown's *Philosophy of Mathematics: An Introduction to a World of Proofs and Pictures* (Routledge 1999) is another lively introduction to this area.

EXERCISES

1. Write a sentence that both uses and mentions the word 'philosophy'. Write a sentence that both uses and mentions some other word. Say where in the two sentences the relevant words are used and where mentioned.

2. 7 7
   How many token numerals are on the previous line? How many type numerals?
   How many natural numbers are less than 10? How many Arabic type numerals are written with one digit?

3. Show how all the integral multiples of 5 (positive and negative) can be paired one-to-one with the natural numbers.

4. Which of the following are subsets of the natural numbers?

   (a) the squares of the natural numbers
   (b) the square roots of the natural numbers

28

(c) the positive whole numbers less than 10 million

(d) the rational numbers

5*. Show that any rational number p/q, with p and q integers, will have a decimal expansion that eventually recurs. (Hint: think about what will happen as you generate the decimal expansion by dividing q into p.)

6*. Show that any decimal number that terminates with a recurring part is equal to some rational number. (Hint: first separate the recurring part, then multiply it by 10^k, where k is the number of digits in the recurring part, then see what happens when you subtract the original recurring part from this number.)

(*Exercises with starred numerals are more difficult.)

3

. . . . .

Orders of Infinity

3.1 Some Harder Stuff

This chapter will be a bit harder.

I regard the issues covered so far as something every educated person should know about. (Maybe my expectations are a bit high—but you get the idea.)

The subject matter of this chapter, however, will be rather more esoteric. I shall explain some points relating to different kinds of infinities. This is not the kind of thing that is normally covered in an introductory philosophy book.

Still, it seems a pity not to go a bit further, now that we have come this far. The material in this chapter is philosophically intriguing, and easy enough to explain in the light of the last two chapters.

3.2 The Numerical Size of Sets

Let us start by thinking about the numerical size of sets, in the sense of how many members they have. (Mathematicians speak here of the 'cardinality' of sets, but I shall stick to the more familiar 'numerical size'.)

In the last chapter we paid attention to ways in which the members of different sets can be paired up one-to-one. In effect, these pairing relationships determine the numerical size of sets. Two sets have the same *number* of members if and only if their respective members can be paired up one-to-one.

This is obvious with finite sets. Two finite sets can be paired up one-to-one if and only if they have the same number of members. Indeed we can think of the natural numbers precisely as ways of characterizing the pairing properties of finite sets. Suppose we group the finite sets by whether their members can be paired up one-to-one. So first we have the empty set, then all the sets with a single member, then all the sets with a pair of members, and so on. We can then think of the natural numbers—0, 1, 2,...—as entities which characterize the common numerical size of the sets in each of these groups. So the number 0 represents the size of the empty set, the number 1 the size of all the single-membered sets, the number 2 the size of all the sets with a pair of members,..., the number 8 the size of all the eight-membered sets, and so on.

Now let us extend this kind of thinking to infinite sets. Suppose we group the infinite sets by seeing whether their members can be paired up one-to-one. So all the denumerable sets will be in one group, for example, and all the sets that can be paired with the real numbers between 0 and 1 in another. Then we can think of all the sets in such a grouping as having the same number of members. So there will be one 'infinite number' that characterizes the denumerable sets, and a distinct and bigger 'infinite number' that characterizes the real numbers between 0 and 1.

If asked, most people would probably say that all infinite sets have the same number of members—infinitely many. What more is there to say about the size of sets which outrun any finite numbering? However, the non-denumerability of the reals has shown us that this reaction is too quick. Given that the real numbers between 0 and 1 cannot be paired up with the natural numbers, we have no choice but to recognize at least two infinite numbers. There is the infinite number that characterizes the denumerable sets, and the distinct and bigger infinite number that characterizes all the sets whose members can be paired up with the real numbers.

In fact we shall see soon enough that there are many more infinite numbers than just these two. Once you start generating infinite numbers it is hard to stop.

3.3 The Reals and the Power Set of the Natural Numbers

It is not hard to show that the set of *real numbers between 0 and 1* has the same numerical size as the set of *all subsets of the natural numbers* (the 'power set' of the natural numbers, in the terminology introduced in Chapter 1).

To see why, suppose we write the real numbers between 0 and 1 in binary notation—e.g. 0.1100101...(Binary notation is simply an alternative way of representing numbers, using powers of 2 where our familiar decimal notation uses powers of 10. See Box 8.) Then we can view each real number as a *recipe* for constructing a subset of the natural numbers: put 0 in the subset if there is a '1' in the first digit of the binary expression; put 1 in the subset if there is a '1' in the second digit of the binary expression;...put n in the subset if there is a '1' in the $(n+1)^{th}$ digit of the binary expression;...

This construction demonstrates that each real number between 0 and 1 can be taken uniquely to determine a subset of the natural numbers. And similarly each subset of the natural numbers uniquely determines a real number between 0 and 1 (...put a '1' for the $(n+1)^{th}$ digit of the binary expression if n is in the subset...). (See Box 8.)

32

Box 8 The Real Numbers and the Power Set of the Natural Numbers

Ordinary decimal notation represents numbers as sums of multiples of powers of 10. So for example:

$107.25 = (1 \times 10^2) + (0 \times 10^1) + (7 \times 10^0) + (2 \times 10^{-1}) + (5 \times 10^{-2})$

Binary notation does the same thing but uses powers of 2 in place of powers of 10. So for example in binary notation the decimally represented 107.25 comes out as:

$1101011.01 = (1 \times 2^6) + (1 \times 2^5) + (0 \times 2^4) + (1 \times 2^3) + (0 \times 2^2) + (1 \times 2^1) + (1 \times 2^0) + (0 \times 2^{-1}) + (1 \times 2^{-2}) = 64 + 32 + 8 + 2 + 1 + 1/4$

Note how binary numerals are always strings of nothing but '1's and '0's (since multiplying by 2 moves you to the next higher power of 2).

So any real number between 0 and 1 can be represented as a (possibly infinite) string of '1's and '0's, for example:

$0.100111001010…$

And this string can then be used as a recipe for constructing a subset of the natural numbers, by including a natural number in the subset iff its matching binary digit is a '1':

The natural numbers:	0	1	2	3	4	5	6	7	8…
Our binary string:	1	0	0	1	1	1	0	0	1…
The resulting subset:	{0,			3,	4,	5,			8…}

Conversely, any subset of the natural numbers can be used as a recipe for constructing a binary numeral between 0 and 1, by putting '1's in the binary string in just those places that correspond to numbers in the subset.

So the *real numbers between 0 and 1* and *the power set of the natural numbers* can be paired up one-to-one, and in this sense compose sets of the same numerical size. (I shall drop the qualification 'between 0 and 1' henceforth, given that the set of *all* real numbers can be shown to have the same numerical size as the set of real numbers between 0 and 1. I leave this as an Exercise.)

Suppose we give the name 'infinity$_0$' to the numerical size of the natural numbers and other denumerable sets, in recognition of the fact that this is the smallest of the infinite numbers.

Now recall that any finite set with n members has a power set with 2^n members—there are 2^n ways of making subsets if we have n members to play with.

Given this, it would seem natural to write the numerical size of the power set of the natural numbers as 2^{infinity_0}.

And by this convention the numerical size of the real numbers will also be 2^{infinity_0}, since they are the same numerical size as the power set of the natural numbers.[1]

---

[1] Don't worry too much about whether it makes sense to raise 2 to the power of infinity$_0$—that is, to multiply 2 by itself infinity$_0$ times. For our present purposes it will be enough to treat '2^{infinity_0}' as nothing more than a usefully mnemonic symbol for the numerical size of the power set of the natural numbers.

Still, for what it is worth, there is a natural way to do arithmetic with infinite numbers, and in this arithmetic we do find that:

$2 \times \text{infinity}_0 = \text{infinity}_0$ and
$\text{infinity}_0 \times \text{infinity}_0 = \text{infinity}_0$
but
$2^{\text{infinity}_0} > \text{infinity}_0$.

3.4 The Continuum Hypothesis

We know that 2^{∞_0} is a distinct and bigger number than ∞_0. Where 2^{∞_0} enumerates the real numbers, ∞_0 enumerates the natural numbers, and Cantor's diagonal argument showed us that the numerical size of the real numbers outruns that of the natural numbers.

But here is an interesting question. Is 2^{∞_0} the *next biggest* infinite number after ∞_0?

There is no guarantee, if you think about it, that this should be so. Maybe there is a kind of infinite set which is intermediate in size between the natural numbers and the real numbers. This would be a set that is too big to be paired up with the natural numbers, but too small for all the real numbers to be paired up with it. If this were so, then the numerical size of this set would be an infinite number that came between ∞_0 and 2^{∞_0}.

Suppose we adopt the convention that '∞_1' names the next biggest infinite number after ∞_0, '∞_2' the next, and so on, for as long as we need to go on. (Mathematicians use '$\aleph_0$', '$\aleph_1$',... for this sequence—pronounced 'aleph-zero', 'aleph-one',... But let us stick to a convention that is easier to follow.)

Our question was whether 2^{∞_0} is the next biggest infinite number after ∞_0. This can now be posed as the question of whether 2^{∞_0} equals ∞_1, or whether it is a distinct and larger infinite number.

The claim that 2^{∞_0} is the same as ∞_1 is the famous '*continuum hypothesis*'. (It is so-called because the real numbers—which are of size 2^{∞_0}, remember—are often thought of as representing a continuous arrangement of points along a line. The 'continuum hypothesis' is thus the hypothesis that the number of such points is the *next* largest infinite number after the number of the natural numbers.)

Amazingly, standard set theory fails to decide this question. Both the continuum hypothesis *and* its denial are consistent with the rest of set theory.

This is very strange. Standard set theory allows us to construct infinite sets as big as the natural numbers, and also ones as big as the real numbers. But it doesn't say whether or not there are any that are in-between in size.

I didn't go into any details at the end of Chapter 1 about the ways in which mathematicians have sought to improve on the failings of naive set theory. But they have devised a number of alternative axiomatic systems that aim to capture the essential features of sets. Yet none of these systems decides the continuum hypothesis. If sets really existed, you would expect there to be a fact of the matter here, and for axiomatic set theory to tell us what it is. The independence of the continuum hypothesis from axiomatic set theory adds weight to the philosophical case against the reality of sets.

(The discovery that the continuum hypothesis is left undecided by standard set theory came relatively late. In 1940 Kurt Gödel showed that the continuum hypothesis itself is consistent with set theory, and in 1963 Paul Cohen showed that the *denial* of this hypothesis is also consistent with set theory.)

3.5 An Infinity of Infinities

There is an infinity of different infinite numbers.

This follows from the fact that the power set of any set S is always of larger numerical size than the set S itself.

This 'power set theorem' can be proved by a generalized version of Cantor's diagonal argument. It shows that any attempt to pair the members of the power set of any set S with the members of S itself will inevitably omit some members of the power set. There are

Box 9 The Power Set Theorem

....

Take any set S and its power set P(S). We want to show that there is no way of pairing the members of P(S) with those of S itself.

Suppose (for the sake of yet another reductio argument) that there is such a pairing.

Members of S:	a	b	c	$\ldots$
Members of P(S):	L	M	N	$\ldots$

Now form a new subset K of S by going through all S's members one by one and sticking them in this new subset if they are *not* in the subset they are paired with. (So the new subset K contains a if and only if a does *not* belong to L, and b if and only if b does *not* belong to M, and so on.)

This new set K will now be a subset of our original S which is *different* from each of the subsets that were initially lined up with members of S.

To see that our constructed K must differ from each of the subsets that were initially lined up with members of S, note that K differs from L with respect to a (it contains a if and only if L doesn't contain it), and differs from M with respect to b (it contains b if and only if M doesn't contain it),...and in general differs from each of the subsets originally paired with the members of S with respect to just that member of S which that subset was originally paired with.

So we have derived a contradiction from the supposition that there is a way of pairing *all* the subsets of S with members of S itself. There can be no such pairing.

(If this reminds you of the 'diagonal' argument from the last chapter, so it should—we've just applied the same trick to subsets that we there applied to decimally represented numbers.)

always too many subsets of S to be paired with the members of S itself. (See Box 9.)

So, just as the power set of the natural numbers is bigger in size than the natural numbers themselves, so also is the power set of *that* set bigger again, and so on.

This guarantees that we have an infinite sequence of infinite numbers, each bigger than the one before. These numbers represent the numerical sizes of the sequence of sets generated from the natural numbers by repeatedly taking power sets.

In line with our earlier convention, it is natural to call these numbers 'infinity$_0$', '2^{infinity_0}', '$2^{2^{\text{infinity}_0}}$', and so on. The rationale for this convention, as before, is that any set with n members has 2^n subsets.

3.6 The Generalized Continuum Hypothesis

To repeat, the sequence of numbers infinity$_0$, 2^{infinity_0}, $2^{2^{\text{infinity}_0}}$, ... enumerates the sequence of sets generated by repeatedly taking power sets of the natural numbers.

Now, analogously to our earlier question of whether or not 2^{infinity_0} is the same as infinity$_1$ (the continuum hypothesis), we can ask how this sequence of numbers 2^{infinity_0}, $2^{2^{\text{infinity}_0}}$, ... relates to the sequence infinity$_1$, infinity$_2$, ... Remember that this latter sequence is simply the sequence of *all* infinite numbers after infinity$_0$ arranged in ascending order.

The '*generalized* continuum hypothesis' states that these two sequences coincide throughout. That is, the *generalized* continuum hypothesis asserts that the sequence infinity$_0$, 2^{infinity_0}, $2^{2^{\text{infinity}_0}}$, ... includes all the infinite numbers. There are no infinite numerical sizes in between those generated by repeatedly taking power sets of the natural numbers. All infinite sets can be paired up one-to-one with one of the power sets generated in this way. (Compare the way that the simple continuum hypothesis said that 2^{infinity_0} coincided with infinity$_1$ and thus that there is no infinite numerical size in between those of the natural numbers and their power set.)

Again, the generalized continuum hypothesis isn't decided by the standard set theory.

FURTHER READING

The last two chapters of Eric Steinhart's *More Precisely: The Math You Need To Do Philosophy* cover the material of this chapter in more detail.

Set Theory and the Continuum Problem by Raymond Smullyan and Mervyn Fitting (Dover revised edition 2010) goes deeper into a lot of the mathematics covered in this chapter.

Adrian Moore's *The Infinite* (Routledge 1990) deals with some of the philosophical issues raised by the notion of infinity.

EXERCISES

1. (a) How many Arabic type numerals are there?
   (b) How many pairs of Arabic type numerals are there?
   (c) How many infinitely long strings of Arabic type numerals are there?

2. Suppose I have a numerical list of all the rational numbers in decimal representation. Why can't I use Cantor's diagonal argument to show that the rationals are non-denumerable?

3. Tighten Cantor's diagonal proof to deal with the problem of alternative decimal representations for the same real number. (Hint: we only get alternative decimal representations when one representation ends with infinitely many nines and the other with infinitely many zeros.)

4. In the text I said that the possibility of representing the real numbers between 0 and 1 in binary form demonstrates that each such number 'can be taken uniquely to determine a subset of the natural numbers'. But in fact this demonstration is not immediate. What is the complication?

5*. Show that all the real numbers can be paired one-to-one with the reals between 0 and 1.

Part II

ANALYTICITY, A PRIORICITY, AND NECESSITY

4

· · • · ·

Kinds of Truths

4.1 Three Distinctions among Truths

There are three interesting ways to divide up the class of true statements. A lot of philosophy depends on the relationships between these divisions.

We can distinguish:

the *analytic* truths from the *synthetic* ones
the *a priori* truths from the *a posteriori* ones
the *necessary* truths from the *contingent* ones.

The first distinction is *semantic*—to do with the meanings of words; the second is *epistemological*—to do with knowledge; and the third is *metaphysical*—to do with the nature of things.

4.2 Analytic and Synthetic

Analytic truths are true by definition. Their truth is guaranteed by the meanings of the words used to state them.

Here are some examples of analytic truths. All triangles have three sides. A vixen is a female fox. If John is Jane's brother, she is his sister.

The truth of these statements falls out of the meanings of the words they contain—'triangles', 'sides', 'vixen', 'female', 'fox', 'brother', 'sister'. The meanings of these words suffice to ensure that the statements are true.

Synthetic truths are those which are not analytic. Their truth depends not just on the meanings of words, but also on the actual facts.

Here are some examples of synthetic truths. Blackbirds eat worms. Bristol is west of Manchester. The sun has eight planets.

The truth of these statements isn't just a matter of meanings, but also of how the non-linguistic world is arranged.

4.3 A Priori and A Posteriori

This distinction is to do with kinds of knowledge rather than the meanings of words.

A true statement is *a priori* if it can be *known* prior to experience of the facts. In principle, you can figure out an a priori truth just by sitting in an armchair with your eyes shut and thinking hard.

The most obvious examples of a priori truths are analytic truths. Anybody who understands the statement *triangles have three sides* won't need to examine any physical triangles to know that this statement is true.

(In a moment we shall consider whether any *other* truths apart from analytic ones can be known a priori.)

A true statement is *a posteriori* if it can only be known as a result of relevant experiences. *Blackbirds eat worms* is an example of an a posteriori truth. There is no way of finding out that this statement is true without making observations.

Note that the requirement for a truth to be a priori is that it *can* be known prior to experience, not that it *must* be known in this way. I might find out that 7 x 6 = 42 by looking at a few actual squares made of seven rows of six pebbles each, counting the total number of pebbles, and inferring the general pattern. But even so this is still an a priori truth, because I *could* have worked it out in my head without making any observations.

One last point about a priority. The idea is not that an a priori statement can be known prior to *any* experience whatsoever—for some experience may be necessary in order to understand the statement in the first place. Rather the requirement is that, once you have enough experience to understand the statement, you don't need any *further* experience to know that it is true. For example, you may need some experience of the world to acquire such concepts as *triangle* and *side*. But anyone who has acquired these concepts can thereby know *triangles have three sides* without any further investigation. By contrast, someone can possess the concepts *blackbird* and *worm* but still not be in a position to know that *blackbirds eat worms*.

4.4 Synthetic A Prioris

Let us leave the third distinction, between necessary and contingent truths, to one side for the minute. First we need to think about the relationship between our first two distinctions, analytic/synthetic and a priori/a posteriori.

Remember that the first distinction is *semantic*—to do with the definitions of words. The second is *epistemological*—to do with acquisition of knowledge. It's not to be taken for granted that these two distinctions line up together.

Above I said that analytic truths provided the most obvious examples of a priori truths. And in general we can see that *any* analytic statement can be known a priori: if the truth of some statement is guaranteed by the meanings of the words it contains, then someone who grasps those meanings will be in a position to work out that it is true.

But are analytic truths the *only* statements that can be known a priori? Or does the realm of things that can be known a priori extend into the synthetic truths? In short, are there any *synthetic a priori* truths?

Many philosophers have thought that there were. Here are some examples of statements that they have thought to be both synthetic and a priori: *all triangles contain 180°, every event has a cause, nothing can be both red and green all over.*

(The traditional 'rationalists'—Descartes, Spinoza, Leibniz—are often said to be distinguished from the 'empiricists'—Locke, Berkeley, Hume—by their belief in synthetic a priori knowledge. But take this with a pinch of salt. While it is certainly true that synthetic a priori knowledge was more important to the Continental rationalists than to the British empiricists, the latter group by no means rejected all examples of this category.)

Perhaps geometry provides the most plausible examples of synthetic a priori knowledge. Consider the statement that *all triangles contain* 180°. This certainly seems to be a synthetic statement. After all, it tells us that if you cut off the three corners of a paper triangle, and then arrange them together, they will make a nice straight line. (See diagram below.) This looks like a substantial fact about the world, not something guaranteed by definition. How could a mere definition make the pieces of paper line up so neatly?

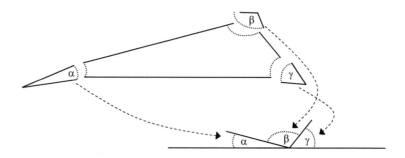

But at the same time it looks as if we can prove this statement a priori, by means of the familiar schoolbook demonstration. (See Box 10.) And this proof seems to tell us beforehand what will happen when we cut out the corners and arrange them together—that is, the proof seems to enable us to know a substantial synthetic fact prior to any experience of the result.

4.5 How is Synthetic A Priori Knowledge Possible?

Here is a question. How can we possibly know a statement to be true prior to experience, if the concepts used to frame it leave it open that it might be false? The truth of such a synthetic statement will depend on the actual facts, as well as on the concepts involved. But how can we know what these facts are, prior to any experience of them?

Before the eighteenth century all philosophers would have had a ready answer. God told us—or, as they would have put it, He has endowed us with a 'natural light of reason' which enables us to identify certain basic truths prior to experience.

That is how we can know the truths of geometry and other such fundamental principles a priori. God has arranged our minds to make these things apparent to us.

Since the middle of the eighteenth century this answer has ceased to be acceptable among mainstream philosophers, even those who believe in God. As a result, synthetic a priori knowledge has become a problematic category for modern philosophy.

At the end of the eighteenth century Immanuel Kant offered a novel defence of synthetic a priori knowledge, arguing that certain assumptions, such as the principles of geometry, must be true of any world which we can experience. But the details of his arguments are not convincing, and in any case his approach arguably requires an idealist metaphysics which equates the world itself with the world as we experience it.

In more recent times a number of thinkers have appealed to biological natural selection to account for synthetic a priori knowledge. Even if God hasn't shaped our minds so as to make certain truths a priori apparent to us, perhaps our biological history has done the job instead.

But there is an obvious difficulty with this biological suggestion. Maybe our biological history predisposes us strongly to certain assumptions about the world. But are these innate assumptions *knowledge*? The trouble is that natural selection is an unreliable informant. It instils beliefs that are practically useful in helping us to survive, but these need not always be true. (For example, humans are arguably innately inclined to believe that physical objects will stop moving unless pushed, in contradiction to modern physics.)

In this respect, natural selection differs from God. Traditional philosophers could be confident that a benevolent God would instil nothing but truths in us ('God is no deceiver' averred Descartes). But the practically useful assumptions bequeathed to us by natural selection can't be taken for granted until they have been subject to further a posteriori investigation.

All in all, I myself am inclined to reject the category of synthetic a priori knowledge and hold that our first two distinctions—analytic/synthetic and a priori/a posteriori—line up together. If something can be known a priori, it must be analytic.

Still, not all contemporary philosophers would agree. The issues are complex and deserve more discussion. But this would take us too far afield here. Fortunately, nothing in what follows will hinge on my rejection of synthetic a priori knowledge.

4.6 Pure and Applied Geometry

If we do reject synthetic a priori knowledge, what about the earlier example of *all triangles contain* 180°? That certainly looked like a good case of synthetic a priori knowledge.

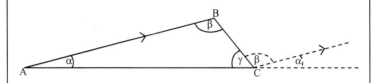

To show a priori that the angles of any triangle add to 180°, first draw a line through C parallel to the line AB. Then note that the two angles labelled β must be equal, as they are alternate angles made when the line CB intersects two parallel lines; and the two angles labelled α must also be equal, as they are corresponding angles made when the line CA intersects two parallel lines. So the three angles inside the triangle must equal the three juxtaposed angles at point C, which together form a straight line, and so sum to 180°.

(Don't be distracted by the visual illustration of this proof. This doesn't mean that the theorem depended on visual experience and was therefore a posteriori. Your visual experience of the illustration played no essential role in your understanding the proof. You didn't measure the angles in the illustration and use this to find out that they added to two 180°. Rather the diagram just helped you follow the proof. In principle you could have understood it while sitting in an armchair and concentrating with your eyes shut.)

However modern physics suggests that this statement, far from being knowable a priori, is not even true. Actual space is 'bent' in such a way that straight lines, defined as the shortest distance between two points, can form triangles whose internal angles do not sum to 180°. (Our earlier 'proof' hinged on the assumption that there is always a single line parallel to another given line through any given point, and that the corresponding and alternate angles made by a line cutting these two parallel lines will be equal. But this assumption need not hold in a 'bent' physical space. See Box 11.)

Some readers might object to this argument against a priori geometry, on the grounds that lines in a bent physical space are not really *straight*. Over two thousand years ago Euclid laid down a set of axioms for geometry. (See Box 12.) These specified a number of properties of points and straight lines, including the postulate that there is always a single line parallel to another given line through any given point. If you stick to these axioms, then the shortest distances between two points in bent spaces will not count as 'straight', since they do not satisfy this 'parallel postulate'. By the same coin, if you do stick to Euclid's axioms, then you can continue to be sure that all triangles made of *Euclidean* straight lines will contain 180°, since by definition Euclidean straight lines do satisfy the parallel postulate, and our earlier proof that triangles will contain 180° can be retained.

However, while this line of thought does yield a kind of a priori geometrical knowledge, this knowledge has now ceased to be *synthetic*. The problem is that, if you insist that nothing will count as a 'straight line' unless it satisfies the axioms of Euclidean geometry, you thereby render all the claims of Euclidean geometry analytic matters of definition, including such theorems as that triangles will contain 180°.

We can distinguish between two ways of understanding geometry. *Applied* geometry is in effect a scientific theory of real physical space. Here we start by specifying how terms like 'point' and 'straight line' refer to items in the real world, and in particular specify that straight lines are the shortest distances between points in real physical space. Once we have defined our terms in this way, it is then a synthetic

Box 11 'Bent' Space

....

The geometry of the surface of a sphere offers a two-dimensional ana-
logue for the way three-dimensional space can be bent. Note how straight
lines (the shortest distances between two points) on the surface of a
sphere will be curved, and how no two of these lines will be parallel in the
sense of never meeting. As a result, our earlier proof does not apply, and
triangles on the surface of a sphere can contain more than 180°. For
example, the angles in the illustrated triangle add up to three right angles,
that is, to 270°.

Of course, we have illustrated the idea of bent space by considering
the two-dimensional surface of a sphere existing inside normal three-
dimensional space in which straight lines still behave as traditionally supposed. But now simply imagine that straight lines in three-dimensional
space behave like the ones on the surface of the sphere. (Which in fact is
roughly what they do, though the distortions are normally too small to be
noticed.)

question whether 'straight lines' so understood satisfy the axioms of Euclidean geometry, and consequently whether all triangles contain 180°. But this synthetic question cannot be answered a priori. We need a posteriori experience of the world, in the form of scientific measurement and experimental results, to tell whether real space is Euclidean. And indeed the a posteriori answer to this question turns out to be 'no'—modern physics tells us that real space does not satisfy the axioms of Euclidean geometry.

Alternatively, we can treat geometry as a purely mathematical construction, with no implications about the structure of physical space. In this kind of *pure* geometry, we start by specifying the axioms something must satisfy by definition to count as a 'point' or 'straight line'— but leave it quite open whether or not real space contains entities of that kind. It can then become a matter of definition that 'straight lines' satisfy the parallel postulate and that all 'triangles' contain 180°. And this definitional knowledge will now be available a priori—but only because it is analytic. Geometry so understood is no longer giving us substantial information about the real world, since its 'straight lines' are no longer guaranteed to correspond to anything in real space. Rather its claims are simply consequences of the way it has defined its terms.

So, whichever way we turn it, geometry fails to deliver any synthetic a priori knowledge. We can treat geometry as a pure mathematical theory, in which case it will be a priori, but only because it is analytic. Or we can treat it as an applied physical theory, in which case it will be synthetic, but now something that can only be decided a posteriori.

Box 12 Euclid's Axioms

Euclid lived in Alexandria during the reign of Ptolemy I (323–283 BC). In his classic textbook the *Elements* he deduced many principles of geometry from five axioms.

Axiom 1. There is a straight line through any two points.

Axiom 2. Any straight line can be extended indefinitely.

Axiom 3. Given any line segment starting at any point, there is a circle with that point as centre and that line segment as radius.

Axiom 4. All right angles are equal.

Axiom 5. There is always a single line parallel to another given line through any given point (where 'parallel' means that the two lines never meet).

The fifth axiom is the interesting one. (In fact Euclid himself gave a slightly more complicated version of this axiom.) From the start mathematicians were uneasy with this fifth axiom—'the parallel postulate'—as it seemed less obvious than the others. For over two thousand years they sought to show that it followed from the other axioms. Finally in the nineteenth century they realized that it isn't in fact required by the other axioms, and indeed that 'non-Euclidean' geometries can be defined by combining the first four axioms with alternatives to Euclid's parallel postulate.

FURTHER READING

In the 1950s the American philosopher W.V.O. Quine mounted an influential attack on the analytic–synthetic distinction in his paper 'Two Dogmas of Empiricism' (reprinted in his collection *From a Logical Point of View*, Harvard University Press second edition 1980).

Quine's attack and other aspects of the distinction are explored in Georges Rey's internet Stanford Encyclopedia of Philosophy entry on 'The Analytic–Synthetic Distinction': <http://plato.stanford.edu/entries/analytic-synthetic>.

There is also a useful Stanford Encyclopedia entry on 'A Priori Knowledge and Justification' by Bruce Russell, which among other things discusses recent attempts to defend synthetic a priori knowledge: <http://plato.stanford.edu/entries/apriori>.

Rationalism, Empiricism and Pragmatism by Bruce Aune (Random House 1970) is a helpful introduction to the historical division between rationalists and empiricists.

Chapter 6 of *Mathematics: A Very Short Introduction* by Timothy Gowers (Oxford University Press 2002) introduces the basic ideas of non-Euclidean geometry.

EXERCISES

1. Give three clear examples of analytic statements, and three of synthetic statements.

2. Which of these would you say was analytic and which synthetic? (In some cases the answer is indeterminate.)

   (a) Vixens are female foxes.
   (b) Leaves contain chlorophyll.
   (c) All spinsters are unmarried.
   (d) Blood transports oxygen.
   (e) Silkworms eat mulberry leaves.
   (f) Energy is always conserved.

(g) Bicycles have two wheels.

(h) All atoms contain nuclei.

3. Explain briefly the difference between being synthetic and being a posteriori.

4. There are obviously some synthetic a posteriori and analytic a priori statements, and some philosophers have defended synthetic a priori statements. What, if anything, is wrong with the idea of an analytic a posteriori statement?

5. Give two examples of statements that have been thought to be examples of synthetic a priori truths.

6. Suppose, for the sake of the argument, that the genes bequeathed to us by natural selection ensure that babies are born believing that *physical objects don't just disappear spontaneously*. Which of the following, if any, are good reasons for denying that the italicized statement is synthetic a priori knowledge?

    (a) The statement is a matter of definition.

    (b) The babies have acquired their belief from experience.

    (c) Natural selection instils plenty of false beliefs in humans.

5

. . ● ● .

Possible Worlds

5.1 Necessity and Contingency

In the last chapter I said that there are three distinctions among truths—analytic/synthetic, a priori/a posteriori, necessary/contingent. And I discussed the first two at length. Let us now consider the last distinction.

A true statement is *necessary* if it could not have been false.
A true statement is *contingent* if it could have been false.

At first sight it may be unclear why this contrast is any different from the a priori/a posteriori distinction. What can it mean to say that a statement *'could not* have been false', apart from saying that there was no room for experience to disprove it because it is a priori? And what can it mean to say that a statement *'could* have been false', apart from that it would have proved false if the evidence had turned out differently?

Certainly many philosophers have agreed that 'necessary' means nothing but 'a priori' and 'contingent' nothing but 'a posteriori'. (If you look in the Index to A.J. Ayer's influential *Language Truth and Logic*, 1936, the entry under 'necessary propositions' simply reads 'see a priori propositions'.)

ANALYTICITY, A PRIORICITY, AND NECESSITY

However, this conflation of the two distinctions is now widely rejected. Over the last few decades, nearly all contemporary philosophers have been persuaded by Saul Kripke's book *Naming and Necessity* that the *metaphysical* distinction between necessary and contingent is different from the *epistemological* distinction between a priori and a posteriori.

According to Kripke, not all necessities are a priori—there are also some *a posteriori necessities*. And not all contingencies are a posteriori––there are also some *contingent a prioris*.

I shall say a lot more about necessity and contingency in this chapter and the next. But let me start by illustrating Kripke's claims that the necessary/contingent and a priori/a posteriori distinctions can come apart, by offering some simple examples of *a posteriori necessities* and *contingent a prioris*.

5.2 A Posteriori Necessities

First for some a posteriori necessities.

My parents were Owen and Constance Papineau. Could I have had different parents? Surely not. A person with different parents would not have been me. So it is necessary that *David Papineau's parents were Owen and Constance Papineau*. But this statement is surely not a priori. You need evidence to know who my parents were. It's not something you can find out just by thinking. So that's one example of an a posteriori necessity.

Here is another. *Hydrogen is made of atoms containing one electron*. This is surely necessary too. *Hydrogen* couldn't have had a different atomic structure. Anything with a different atomic structure wouldn't be hydrogen. But this statement too is obviously a posteriori. Physicists didn't figure out the structure of hydrogen by sitting in an armchair. They needed to perform a great number of detailed experiments and observations.

Perhaps the most obvious examples of a posteriori necessities are simple identities involving proper names. *Marilyn Monroe is Norma*

Jeane Baker. This again is necessary. Marilyn Monroe couldn't not have been Norma Jeane Baker. That would require her somehow not to have been herself, which would be absurd. But *Marilyn Monroe is Norma Jeane Baker* is not a priori. Somebody could understand this statement perfectly well and yet not know it is true. (Imagine someone who grew up with Norma Jeane but lost touch with her, and had heard of Marilyn Monroe but not seen any of the films.)

5.3 A Priori Contingencies

Now for the converse category of a priori contingencies.

Kripke's own example involved the platinum rod in Paris that once defined the metre as a unit of length. He pointed out that, given this definition, it was a priori that *the Paris platinum rod is one metre long*. We could know this without further ado, given that the rod provided the standard for determining what a metre is. But at the same time this statement seems contingent. That selfsame rod might well have been shorter than a metre, if its manufacturer had chosen to make it so.

If there seems an element of trickery about this example, here is another example that makes it clearer what is going on.

Suppose we are discussing the history of inventions, and are particularly interested in what kind of person might have invented the zip. But we get bored having to say 'the inventor of the zip' all the time, so we adopt the name 'Julius' to refer to the inventor of the zip, whoever he or she might have been. Now given this convention, the statement that *Julius invented the zip (assuming it had a single inventor[1]) is*

---

[1] The qualification 'assuming it had a single inventor' is to cover such possibilities as that a team invented it, or perhaps it happened by chance. I'm going to drop the qualification henceforth in the interests of simplicity—it makes no difference to the argument. (The example of Julius is due to the Oxford philosopher Gareth Evans (1946–1980).)

ANALYTICITY, A PRIORICITY, AND NECESSITY

surely a priori. We don't need to investigate the world to make sure that it was Julius who invented the zip.

The statement that *Julius invented the zip* may be a priori, but it is surely not necessary. Julius might have been dropped on his head when little, and grown up too stupid to invent the zip. Or an unhappy love affair might have made him join the French Foreign Legion before he made his breakthrough. The statement that *Julius invented the zip* could well have been false, if things had turned out differently. So this statement is both a priori and contingent.

5.4 Possibility and Necessity

It will be helpful to bring in the idea of a statement being *possible*. A statement is possible if it *might* be true.

Both true statements and false statements can be possible. In this sense, both *David Papineau is a philosopher* and *David Papineau is a lawyer* are possible. The first is true and the second false, but neither is ruled out by the nature of things. I could have been a lawyer, if my life had taken a different course.

Possibility can then be contrasted with necessity. A necessary statement is one which *has* to be true. It couldn't be false. For example, *seven is a prime number*. There are no circumstances in which this statement would be false.

I started this chapter by drawing a contrast between necessary and contingent *truths*. A contingent truth is a true statement that is not necessarily true.

The contrast between necessity and possibility is different. A statement can be possible without being true. The necessity/possibility contrast thus marks a division among *all* statements, rather than just among the *true* statements.

(In terms of possibility, a contingent truth can thus be defined as a statement which is true but could possibly have been false.)

Necessity and possibility have a neat relationship. A statement is necessary if and only if its negation is not possible. That is: necessarily *p* iff *not* possibly *not-p*.

It works the other way round too. A statement is possible iff its negation is not necessary. That is: possibly *p* iff *not* necessarily *not-p*.

Logicians use the symbol '□' (called 'box') for *necessarily*, and ◊' ('diamond') for *possibly*.

Then we can write:

□ p iff not ◊ not-p

and

◊ p iff not □ not-p.

(If you'd like help remembering which is which, think of the box as solid, stable, it couldn't be different; the diamond by contrast is balanced on its tip, and so could go either way.)

5.5 Possible Worlds

It helps to think of these matters in terms of 'possible worlds'.

A possible world is a fully specific way the world might be. Imagine a world which is just as detailed as the actual world, but which differs from the actual world in various respects.

In this context 'world' means the whole universe, not just the planet Earth. Other possible worlds aren't faraway planets within the actual universe. Rather they are alternative universes, with their own space and time. Many of them will contain their own stars and planets and so on—though some of them won't have stars and planets at all.

So there are (many) possible worlds where it is true that *David Papineau is a lawyer*, or that *donkeys talk* or that *the sun has twenty planets* or even that *there is no force of gravity* or that *the whole universe is nothing but mud and telepathic worms are the only intelligent life*. (See Box 13).

5.6 Necessity and Possibility in terms of Worlds

It is easy to explain necessity and possibility in terms of truth at possible worlds:

Necessarily p iff p is true at *all* possible worlds
Possibly p iff p is true at *at least one* possible world

Note how neatly this way of understanding necessity and possibility explains our two earlier equivalences.

(I) Necessarily p iff not possibly not-p.

In terms of possible worlds, the left-hand side of this equivalence now means *p is true at all possible worlds* and the right-hand side means *there are no possible worlds where not-p is true*. The equivalence is now obvious.

And similarly with:

(II) Possibly p iff not necessarily not-p.

The left-hand side now means *p is true at at least one possible world* and the right-hand side means *it's not the case that not-p is true at all possible worlds*. Again the equivalence is obvious.

5.7 Constraints on Possible Worlds

It would be nice to be more specific about which worlds are possible.

As Box 13 explains, possible worlds aren't constrained to respect ordinary scientific principles or anything like that. There are possible worlds containing nothing but two dragons fighting for five minutes.

However, possible worlds do obey some constraints.

For a start, there are no possible worlds which violate logic or definitions.

So there are no possible worlds where it is true that *the earth has a moon and does not have a moon* or that *all cats are black and some are not black* or that *triangles have four sides* or that *John is both taller and shorter than Jim*. These worlds would be inconsistent with logic or definitions. (What about the possible worlds where it is true that *Julius does not invent the zip*—because he was dropped on his head when little, say? Aren't they ruled out by logic and definitions, if Julius is defined as the inventor of the zip? I'll come back to this in the next chapter.)

In addition to restrictions that derive from logic and definitions, possible worlds must also respect the *essential properties* of things, such as facts of identity, origin, and constitution, even when these are not required by logic or definitions.

So there are no possible worlds where it is true that *Marilyn Monroe is not Norma Jeane Baker* (a fact of identity) or that *David Papineau has parents other than Owen and Constance* (a fact of origin) or that *hydrogen is made of atoms with two electrons* (a fact of constitution). These worlds may not be ruled out by logic or definitions, but they are not 'meta-physically' possible. They are inconsistent with the nature of the entities at issue.

Box 13 The Reality of Possible Worlds

Do other possible worlds really exist?

Some scientists argue that quantum mechanics and cosmology provide evidence for other 'branches of reality' apart from the one we live in. But these scientifically motivated alternative universes are different from the philosophers' 'possible worlds'. There are far fewer of them and they are all constrained by the actual laws of physics. Scientists speak of them as together comprising the one actual 'multiverse'.

The 'possible worlds' of the philosophers, by contrast, include a far wider range of alternatives, including worlds with different scientific laws and disparate origins, and indeed worlds which display no order at all. In this sense there are 'possible worlds', for example, which contain nothing but two dragons fighting for five minutes.

The American philosopher David Lewis (1941–2001) was a full-blooded realist about all these possible worlds. According to Lewis, all possible worlds are just as real and concrete as the actual world. The only sense in which this world is 'actual' is that it is the one we happen to be in.

Most philosophers, however, regard this view as untenable, and deny that other possible worlds have the same kind of reality as the actual world. Some equate possible worlds with sets of statements or with rearrangements of actual objects and properties. Others regard them as useful fictions.

Still, whatever view we take of possible worlds, it is uncontroversial that talking about them can be a great help in understanding the structure of necessity and possibility.

5.8 Essential Properties

I said that possible worlds must respect the essential properties of things. Some properties of things are *essential*, others are *accidental*.

I am only accidentally a philosopher and only accidentally live in London. I might have been a lawyer living in Los Angeles.

But I am essentially the child of Owen and Constance Papineau. If you posit a being with different parents, it cannot be me. Similarly, I am essentially a human being. I could not have been a fish or even a chimpanzee. A being of a different species would not be me.

Again, hydrogen essentially has atoms with one electron, but is only accidentally used to make bombs, and Marilyn Monroe is essentially identical to Norma Jeane Baker, but is only accidentally a film star.

Statements ascribing essential properties to things are necessary truths. It is necessary that *David Papineau is the child of Owen and Constance Papineau*, and necessary that *David Papineau is a human being*.

Note however that the necessity of these statements does not make *me* a necessary being. It is certainly possible that I might have failed to exist—suppose, for example, that my parents had never met each other. I am a contingent being, not a necessary one—I exist, but might not have.

Necessities like *David Papineau is a human being* show that we need to be a bit careful about our earlier equation of necessity with 'truth at all possible worlds'. After all, the statement that *David Papineau is a human being* won't be true at those possible worlds where it is false that I exist.

The best way to deal with this is to recognize that necessary truths ascribing essential properties to contingent beings are implicitly conditional. If you think about it, what is really necessary is that *if David Papineau exists, then he is a human being*, not that *David Papineau (exists and) is a human being.* As we have seen, the latter claim could easily have been false—for example, if my parents had never met.

5.9 The Nature of Necessity

By now some readers might be starting to feel suspicious of the whole apparatus of necessity and possibility. Who makes the rules about what is necessary and what is merely possible? Why are my parents and my species necessary to me, but not my being a philosopher and my location? More generally, what does it really *mean* to say that some truths are necessary and others only contingent?

This is a deep and difficult subject, about which it is hard to say anything without being controversial. Indeed there are philosophers who would dispute some of the examples of essential properties I have given so far. I shall return to this issue at the end of the next chapter. But at this stage it may be helpful to make some brief general remarks.

Modal claims—that is, claims about what is necessary and possible—are arguably grounded in our practice of reasoning about non-actual scenarios. It is very common, outside philosophy as much as within it, to think about how things would be if reality were different in various respects. Such thinking is important in many ways—in constructing plans, in ascribing responsibility, in learning from experience, and so on. Would a reduction in taxes cause inflation? Could Bush have invaded Iraq without Tony Blair's support? Would Johnny have got better if he hadn't taken the pills? Could life have evolved if there had been no force of gravity? (In Chapter 8 we shall look briefly at the 'subjunctive conditional' statements which play a central role in this kind of reasoning.)

Now, we can think of modal facts as constraints governing reasoning about non-actual scenarios. Necessary facts are those which *must* be respected in such reasoning. Possible facts are those which *may* be entertained in such reasoning. (Thus it makes sense to consider what would have happened to me if I had studied law, but not what would have happened to me if I had been a fish or conceived by different parents.)

This might not tell us very much about modal facts, without some further account of non-actual reasoning. (What is such reasoning *about*, after all?) But at least we can say this much: modal facts mark out the limits of the space we explore in non-actual reasoning. This kind of reasoning deals with scenarios that are not actual, but it draws the line at scenarios that are not possible.

5.10 Different Kinds of Possibility

Isn't it impossible that a donkey should talk, or that pigs should fly, or that a human being should run a mile in one minute?

But this is only true in a different sense of impossibility. Possible worlds where donkeys talk, or pigs fly, or humans run one-minute miles, are not ruled out by logic or definitions or the essential properties of things. So, for all that has been said so far, these things are possible. When people say that these things are impossible, what they mean is rather that they are not *naturally* possible.

We can understand 'natural possibility' as requiring possibility *plus* consistency with the laws of nature. (Think of the laws of nature as the general truths that science aims to uncover.) Talking donkeys, flying pigs, and one-minute miles are not naturally possible because they are inconsistent with the actual laws of nature. But they are possible in an absolute sense, because there are possible worlds where different laws of nature do allow such things.

In line with this, we can define the *naturally possible* worlds as those absolutely possible worlds where the actual laws of nature obtain. A naturally

ANALYTICITY, A PRIORICITY, AND NECESSITY

possible statement is then one which is true at at least one naturally possible world, and a naturally necessary statement is one which is true at all naturally possible worlds. Trivially, then, the laws of nature themselves are naturally necessary, even if they are not absolutely necessary.

Just as we can define 'natural possibility' as absolute possibility plus consistency with the laws of nature, so we can define 'geographical possibility' as absolute possibility plus consistency with the truths of geography, 'moral possibility' as absolute possibility plus consistency with the truths of morality, and so on.

In what follows these narrower kinds of possibility will not be at issue. From now on all talk of possibility and necessity should be understood as referring to absolute possibility and necessity.

FURTHER READING

Modern work on necessity and possibility starts with Saul Kripke's book *Naming and Necessity* (Blackwell 1980). (In fact the main text was published a decade earlier in article form, after two of Kripke's colleagues transcribed three lectures he delivered without notes at Princeton in 1970. The book simply adds an Introduction to the transcript of the lectures.)

Naming and Necessity is itself very readable. For an overview and some criticisms of Kripke's views, see *Kripke* by Christopher Hughes (Oxford University Press 2004).

David Lewis' realism about possible worlds is explained and defended in his *On the Plurality of Worlds* (Blackwell 1986).

EXERCISES

1. Which of these truths are necessary and which contingent?

    (a) All triangles have three sides.
    (b) There are no snakes in Ireland.
    (c) Water is H_2O.
    (d) My car is blue.
    (e) My car is blue or not blue.
    (f) George Eliot is Mary Ann Evans.
    (g) David Papineau is a philosopher.
    (h) George Eliot wrote *Middlemarch*.

2. Give an example of (a) an a posteriori necessity, (b) an a priori necessity, (c) an a priori contingency, (d) an a posteriori contingency.

3. Which of the following fall into which of the four categories specified in question 2?

    (a) Squares have four sides.
    (b) David Papineau lives in London.
    (c) Cary Grant is Archie Leach.
    (d) The Paris platinum rod is one metre long.
    (e) Prince Charles is the son of Queen Elizabeth and Prince Philip.
    (f) It is raining or it is not raining.
    (g) Julius (as defined in section 5.3) invented the zip.
    (h) London is the capital of Great Britain.

4. Which of these implications are correct? (In each case explain your answer in terms of what the first and second clauses respectively require of the possible worlds p is true in.)

   (a) If p is necessary, it is possible.
   (b) If p is possible, it is necessary.
   (c) If p is necessary, it is not possible.
   (d) If p is true, it is possible.
   (e) If p is false, it is possible.
   (f) If p is not necessary, it not possible.
   (g) If p is not possible, not-p is necessary.

5. For each of the following impossibilities, say whether they are ruled out (i) by logic and definitions or (ii) by the essential properties of things.

   (a) Some birds fly and all birds don't fly.
   (b) Water is sodium chloride.
   (c) Archie Leach is not Cary Grant.
   (d) David Papineau has parents other than Owen and Constance Papineau.
   (e) It is raining and it is not raining.
   (f) Some squares have three sides.

6. For each of the following false statements, say whether it is (i) naturally possible, (ii) absolutely but not naturally possible, (iii) neither.

   (a) Some birds fly and all birds don't fly.
   (b) Tony Curtis is Kirk Douglas.
   (c) Some pigs fly.
   (d) Hydrogen atoms contain two electrons.
   (e) David Papineau is a lawyer.
   (f) The earth revolves once an hour.
   (g) David Papineau has run ten miles in under ten hours.
   (h) David Papineau has run ten miles in under ten minutes.

6

• • • • •

Naming and Necessity

6.1 Two Readings of Statements of Necessity

Consider a statement like

(1) The inventor of the zip necessarily invented the zip.

This can be read two ways.

(2) It is necessary that the inventor of the zip invented the zip.

This says that, in any possible world, the person who invented the zip, whoever that might be, invented the zip. (2) is true. It would violate logic for there to be a world within which the person who invented the zip did not invent the zip.

(3) The inventor of the zip necessarily invented the zip.

Now we are focusing on the actual inventor of the zip, the person who happened to invent the zip in the actual world. The question is whether he or she necessarily invented the zip. It is clear that the answer is negative. The actual inventor of the zip could well have been dropped on his or her head as a child, say, and so grown up too stupid to invent the zip, or gone off to join the French Foreign Legion. Whoever invented

ANALYTICITY, A PRIORICITY, AND NECESSITY

the zip, it was not essential to their nature that they did so. It is quite possible that the actual inventor of the zip should have failed to invent the zip.

6.2 Scope Distinctions

This kind of ambiguity is called a *scope* distinction.
Consider the statement *every girl loves a sailor.*
This can be read either as saying

For every girl, there is a sailor (possibly different for each girl) whom that girl loves,

or as

There is a certain sailor whom every girl loves.

In more explicitly logical notation, the contrast is between

(For each girl x)(there exists a sailor y such that)(x loves y),

and

(There exists a sailor y such that)(for each girl x)(x loves y).

In the first case we say that the expression '(For each)' has *wide scope* and the expression '(there exists)' has *narrow scope*. In the second case this is reversed.
Now return to our two readings of *the inventor of the zip necessarily invented the zip.*
The first was

(2) It is necessary that the inventor of the zip invented the zip.

In more explicit notation:

(Necessarily)(the inventor of the zip)(invented the zip)

So here we can say that the prefix '(Necessarily)' has wide scope, while the description '(the inventor of the zip)' has narrow scope.

The other reading was

(3) The inventor of the zip necessarily invented the zip.

More explicitly:

(The inventor of the zip)(necessarily)(invented the zip).

Now it is the description '(The inventor of the zip)' that has wide scope, while the prefix '(necessarily)' has narrow scope.

6.3 Julius and the Inventor of the Zip

Attentive readers may be puzzled at this point. Recall the name 'Julius' from the last chapter defined as 'the inventor of the zip'. I said there that *Julius invented the zip* is clearly contingent (given that Julius could have been dropped on his head when little …). That is, I said that this statement is definitely false:

(4) Julius necessarily invented the zip.

But—and this is the puzzle—how come this is definitely false, rather than ambiguous between a true and false reading? I started this chapter by observing that the statement (1)—*the inventor of the zip necessarily invented the zip*—is ambiguous between a true and false reading. But surely (4) and (1) must mean the same. After all 'Julius' was explicitly defined as 'the inventor of the zip'. So, given that (1) is ambiguous, why isn't (4) similarly ambiguous? But, on the face of it, (4) is indeed definitely false, not ambiguous.

However, there is a difference between (4) and (1). Even though 'Julius' was defined as the inventor of the zip, so to speak, it remains the case that 'Julius' is a *proper name*, where 'the inventor of the zip' is a *description*.

And this difference explains why (4) is definitely false, while (1) is ambiguous. The fact that 'Julius' is a proper name *forces* us to read (4) as about the person who invented the zip in the actual world, and so as akin to the reading of (1) in which 'the inventor of the zip' has wide scope and 'necessarily' has narrow scope. While (1)—*the inventor of the zip necessarily invented the zip*—can be read in two ways, depending on whether we ascribe a wide or narrow scope to 'necessarily', (4)—*Julius necessarily invented the zip*—can only be understood one way, as saying (falsely) of Julius that he or she necessarily invented the zip.

6.4 Rigid Designators

Proper names are terms for people, places, and other important objects—like 'David Papineau', 'London', 'Titanic', and so on. They are typically written with capital letters, and their function is to pick out some individual, rather than to convey descriptive information about it.

This is why in modal statements they always work like descriptions with wide scope. (A *modal* statement is any statement saying that something is necessary or possible.) We cannot help but understand modal statements made using proper names as first identifying some object and then saying what is necessary or possible about *it*. (And this remains the case even when, as with 'Julius', the proper name has explicitly been attached to its bearer with the help of some description.)

Words that always work like this in modal statements are called '*rigid designators*'. Proper names are the most obvious examples of rigid designators. But there are arguably other species of this genus. In particular, many philosophers think that names of scientific categories—like 'hydrogen', 'water', 'tiger', and so on—are also rigid designators.

It is sometimes said that 'rigid designators have their referents necessarily'. But this can be confusing. The idea is not that the *word* 'David

Papineau' necessarily names me. That is obvious false—I could easily have been given a different name.

Rather the idea is that the name 'David Papineau' (as used in the actual world) picks out a certain actual individual (namely me) and in modal statements must still be understood as talking about that same individual and saying what is necessary or possible about *it*.

6.5 The Causal Theory of Reference

The idea of rigid designation was introduced by Saul Kripke in the book *Naming and Necessity* mentioned earlier. Part of the purpose of the book was to show that proper names are rigid designators. But Kripke also defended another view about proper names—normally referred to as the 'causal theory of reference' (though Kripke himself never claimed that this view added up to a 'theory').

We need to be careful not to muddle up this causal theory with the thesis that proper names are rigid designators.

The 'causal theory of reference' is a theory of how names get related to their bearers in the actual world. It is opposed to the more traditional 'description theory', according to which a name refers to whatever entity satisfies the descriptions people associate with the name. (To illustrate the description theory, take the name 'Ferdinand Magellan'; nearly everybody associates this name first and foremost with the description 'the first man to circumnavigate the globe'; so according to the description theory the name 'Ferdinand Magellan' refers to whomever was that first circumnavigator.)

Kripke argued that the description theory gives the wrong account of how proper names get their references fixed. Names don't normally get hooked on to their bearers by being associated with a set of descriptions. It's much simpler. There is some original occasion where the individual in question is first named (most obviously, the baptism of a child). Thereafter the name spreads through the community. As a result, all those who later use the name will be referring to the individual origin-ally dubbed with it, even if those later users lack descriptive knowledge of that individual. (The 'causal' in 'the causal theory of reference' alludes to the way the name spreads *causally* though the community, with later users acquiring the name through causal contact with earlier users.)

This is not the place to adjudicate between the description and causal theories of reference. Kripke makes a strong case for the latter, but not all philosophers are convinced. (To get a sense of Kripke's case, note that Ferdinand Magellan didn't in fact circumnavigate the globe, having got himself killed when he was half-way round. How-ever, if the description theory were correct, it's not clear how what I have just said could be true.)

6.6 Rigidity and the Causal Theory

The point I want to stress here is that the causal theory of reference is not the same as the doctrine that proper names are rigid designators. The former is a thesis about the way names get attached to their bear-ers in the actual world. The latter is a thesis about the way that names behave in modal statements. The two theses are distinct.

This point is made graphic by the example of 'Julius'. If you think about it, 'Julius' is a name that is cooked up to fit the description the-ory of reference. The description theory is true of 'Julius', even if it is false of other proper names. But this does not stop 'Julius' being a rigid designator. In any modal statement it must still be read as referring to the *actual* inventor of the zip and saying what is necessary or possible about *that person*. So 'Julius''s status as a rigid designator does not depend on its conforming to the causal theory of reference. It just fol-lows from the fact that 'Julius' is a proper name.

The example of 'Julius' shows how proper names could be rigid designators *even if* the description theory of reference were true. Rigid designation doesn't require the causal theory of reference.

However, there is arguably a connection between rigid designation and the theory of reference in the other direction. Even if rigid designation doesn't require the causal theory of reference, maybe the causal theory of reference requires rigid designation.

A referring term is *non-rigid* if what it refers to at different possible worlds is independent of what it refers to at the actual world. So, for example, the explicit description 'the first mammal on the moon' can be read as referring to whichever mammal was first on the moon in different possible worlds. When we are considering the actual world, it refers to Neil Armstrong. But when we consider the possibility where the Russians send their original space dog to the moon and not just into orbit, it refers to that dog. And in general, in considering any possible world, the description can be read as referring to whatever mammal was first on the moon in that world.

Note how this kind of non-rigid reference requires that the referring term in question has some descriptive content that can be satisfied by different objects in different possible worlds. Without such a descriptive content, there wouldn't be any question of understanding the term as referring to whatever satisfies some given description in different possible worlds.

So, if proper names have their references fixed causally, and not by association with descriptions, it is hard to see how they *could* behave in this non-rigid way. They have no option, so to speak, but to refer rigidly, in all modal contexts, to the thing that they name in the actual world.

6.7 De Dicto and De Re

In the last chapter I noted that there are two kinds of limits to possibility. First there is the requirement that possible worlds should respect logic and definitions: there are no possible worlds that are logically contradictory. Second there is the requirement that possible worlds should respect the essential properties of things: it is not possible that things should lack their essential properties.

Corresponding to these two limits are two kinds of modal statements. There are '*de dicto*' modal statements, which answer to the requirements of logic and definitions, and there are '*de re*' modal statements, which are concerned with whether specific things have certain properties essentially or not.

De dicto modal statements are thus ones which contain no rigid designators, and in which the 'necessarily' or 'possibly' prefix takes wide scope. Examples of this category include:

(Necessarily)(the first mammal on the moon)(was human)
(Possibly)(the cleverest girl)(has the richest parents)
(Necessarily)(the inventor of the zip)(invented the zip)
(Possibly)(there is a triangle with four sides).

Statements like these are traditionally called '*de dicto*'—of the word—because the truth or falsity of these statements hinges on the descriptions involved, and not on what those descriptions refer to in the actual world.

De re modal statements, by contrast, are those in which the 'necessarily' or 'possibly' prefix takes narrow scope, or which contain rigid designators. Examples of this category include:

(The first mammal on the moon)(necessarily)(was human)
(The inventor of the zip)(possibly)(did not invent the zip)
Necessarily Julius invented the zip
Possibly David Papineau is the son of Franklin and Eleanor Roosevelt.

Statements like these are traditionally called '*de re*'—of the thing—because now we are focussing on some specific thing in the actual world, and asking whether *it* necessarily or possibly has some property, however that thing might be described.

6.8 Necessary and A Priori Again

As long as we stick to de dicto statements, then we can expect necessity and a priority to line up together. For a de dicto necessary statement to be true, all possible worlds must conform to some purely descriptive requirement. But how could this be so, unless the descriptive requirement were guaranteed to be true by logic and definitions? So in such cases the statement will be knowable a priori. (Consider, for instance, such requirements as that *the inventor of the zip invented the zip*, or that *either the earth has a moon or it doesn't*, or that *triangles have three sides...*)

But once we switch to de re statements, then necessity and a priority can come apart. This is the source of Kripke's examples of a priori contingencies and a posteriori necessities.

Let us first consider a priori contingencies. These arise when we identify the relevant entity in a way that makes it *a priori* that it has some *accidental* property. For example, it is a priori that the inventor of the zip, and indeed Julius, invented the zip. But inventing the zip is not a necessary property of that person.

Now take a posteriori necessities. These arise when we identify something in a way that makes it *a posteriori* that it has some *essential* property. For example, it is a posteriori that the first mammal on the moon was human, or that David Papineau is the son of Owen and Constance Papineau. But membership of the human species is necessary to the first mammal on the moon (namely, Neil Armstrong), and similarly my parenthood is necessary to me.

Of course, we can also identify things in a way that makes it a posteriori that they have an accidental property (David Papineau is a philosopher) and a priori that they have an essential property (the first human on the moon was human). The point is that the accidentality or essentiality of a property ascribed to some entity is *independent* of whether or not we identify that entity in a way that makes it a priori that it possesses that property.

80 ANALYTICITY, A PRIORICITY, AND NECESSITY

We can now clear up a question left hanging earlier. Why is there a possible world where it is true that *Julius did not invent the zip*? This statement is a priori contradictory—its falsity is guaranteed by the definition of 'Julius'. So shouldn't any such possibility be ruled out?

Well, there is certainly no possible world in which somebody both does and doesn't invent the zip. That would contradict logic. But that's not the kind of possibility required to make it true that *Julius* did not invent the zip. And there is no contradiction in this latter possibility, precisely because it is perfectly possible that Julius lack the property of inventing the zip, even though we happen to use this accidental property to identify him or her in this world.

Look at it like this. Even though we identify Julius in this world as the person who invented the zip, we throw away this information, so to speak, when we consider the possible world where it is true that he or she doesn't invent the zip. The way we identify Julius in this world a priori guarantees the actual-world truth of *Julius invented the zip*. But because this accidental fact about Julius isn't carried over to other possible worlds, there can be some where it is false that Julius invented the zip.

6.9 A Limit to Scepticism about A Posteriori Necessity

I have taken it throughout this chapter and the last that there is a distinction between accidental and essential properties of things. My parentage is essential to me, but not my profession. Its atomic structure is essential to hydrogen, but not the fact that it can be used to make bombs.

However, I have said little about the basis for this distinction, beyond my brief remarks at the end of the last chapter about reasoning about non-actual scenarios.

Some philosophers are unsure about the distinction between essential and the accidental properties, and accordingly tend to be uneasy about examples of a posteriori necessities. So a common response to such examples of a posteriori necessity as *David Papineau's parents are Owen and Constance Papineau* or *hydrogen is made of atoms containing one electron* is to query whether their parents really are necessary to humans, or whether atomic structure really is necessary to chemical elements.

(Imagine a being like me, with just the same genetic make-up, but where my conception involved people other than Owen and Constance. Why wouldn't that be a world in which *David Papineau* had different parents? Or imagine a world otherwise like ours but where subatomic structure didn't involve electrons orbiting nuclei. Why wouldn't that be a world where *hydrogen* isn't made of atoms containing one electron?)

However, there are limits to this kind of scepticism about a posteriori necessity. While there is perhaps room for doubt about the necessity of parentage and atomic constitution, it is very hard to deny that true identity claims made using different proper names are a posteriori necessities.

Consider this argument.

(1) Necessarily Norma Jeane Baker = Norma Jeane Baker.

(2) Since proper names are rigid designators, this is a de re claim about the actual Norma Jeane Baker, saying that she necessarily has the property of being identical to Norma Jeane Baker.

(3) But Norma Jeane Baker = Marilyn Monroe.

(4) So, by the Indiscernibility of Identicals (see Box 14), every property of Norma Jeane Baker is a property of Marilyn Monroe and vice versa.

82

(5) So in particular, Marilyn Monroe must share with Norma Jeane Baker the property identified in (2), of being necessarily identical to Norma Jeane Baker.

(6) So necessarily Marilyn Monroe = Norma Jeane Baker.

And this last claim then gives us an a posteriori necessity, since it is certainly not a priori that Marilyn Monroe is identical to Norma Jeane Baker.

Clearly this argument can be repeated, with any true identity statement involving two different names, to make a case that any such statement is necessary and a posteriori.

Note how this argument for a posteriori necessities only carries force with identity claims, and not with other putative examples of de re essential truths like claims about origin or constitution. This is because the first premise would be contentious if it involved some claim about origin or constitution.

Thus suppose that we started a version of the above argument with:

(7) Necessarily Norma Jeane Baker is the child of Norma Jeane Baker's parents

and then proceeded as before to conclude with the putative a posteriori necessity that

(8) Necessarily Marilyn Monroe is the child of Norma Jeane Baker's parents.

The trouble with this latter argument is that sceptics will query (7) by questioning whether parenthood is really a de re necessary property.

By contrast, there seems little room to query the original premise (1), that necessarily Norma Jeane Baker = Norma Jeane Baker.

Box 14 The Indiscernibility of Identicals and the Identity of Indiscernibles

....

The principle of the Indiscernibility of Identicals says that if two things are identical they must share all their properties:

(For all things x, y)(if x = y, then (for all properties F)(x has F iff y has F))

This *Indiscernibility of Identicals* must be distinguished from its converse, the *Identity of Indiscernibles*. The latter principle says that if two things share all their properties, then they must be identical:

(For all things x, y)(if (for all properties F)(x has F iff y has F), then x = y)

There is no dispute about the former Indiscernibility of Identicals. A thing is what it is. If it has some property, then it has that property, however it is named. A rose by any other name would smell as sweet.

The Identity of Indiscernibles is far more controversial. Note that when it comes to evaluating this disputable thesis, it matters what counts as a property. If we include facts about what objects you are identical to among your relevant properties, then the Identity of Indiscernibles is indeed trivially true. Any *a* and *b* will automatically have distinct 'properties', in that the first but not the second will be *identical to a*, while the second but not the first will be *identical to b*, which makes it automatic that in order to be different you must be 'discernible'.

However, if we exclude such 'identity properties', then the Indiscernibility of Identicals becomes a substantial thesis, and indeed a very doubtful one. As the philosopher Max Black once asked, could there not be a universe which contained nothing but two perfect spheres of the same size, which would thus share all their properties yet remain distinct?

ANALYTICITY, A PRIORICITY, AND NECESSITY

FURTHER READING

The first resource for rigid designation and the causal view of reference is once more Kripke's own *Naming and Necessity* (Blackwell 1980).

There is a useful entry on theories of reference by Marga Reimer in the Stanford Encyclopedia of Philosophy: <http://plato.stanford.edu/entries/reference>.

The Stanford Encyclopedia entry on essential and accidental properties by Teresa Robertson is also helpful: <http://plato.stanford.edu/entries/essential-accidental>.

Penelope Mackie's *How Things Might Have Been: Individuals, Kinds, and Essential Properties* (Oxford University Press 2006) goes into greater detail on this topic.

Chapter 5 of Mark Sainsbury's *Logical Forms* (Blackwell second edition 2001) contains a great deal of useful material on modality, including a discussion of the distinction between *de re* and *de dicto* claims.

David Lewis' *On the Plurality of Worlds* (Blackwell 1986) is again relevant. It should be noted that Lewis' full-blooded realism about possible worlds makes some room for him to reject the argument from the Indiscernibility of Identicals in section 6.9.

EXERCISES

1. Show how the following statements are ambiguous by using brackets to write two unambiguous sentences that gives a plausible reading of each.

   (a) Every boy hates a teacher.
   (b) A teacher hates every boy.
   (c) Necessarily the first mammal on the moon was human.
   (d) Necessarily the tallest person in Britain is shorter than no one in Britain.
   (e) The head of the King's College London philosophy department might not have been head of the King's College London philosophy department.
   (f) The inventor of the zip couldn't not have invented the zip.

2. For each of your last four answers to the previous question, say which of your two readings is true and which false. (For this and the following exercises, put to one side any doubts you may have about the examples of de re necessities used in this chapter.)

3. Which of these are 'de re' statements, and which 'de dicto'?

   (a) (The inventor of the zip) (might not have invented the zip).
   (b) (It might have been the case that) (the inventor of the zip did not invent the zip).
   (c) (It might have been the case that) (Julius did not invent the zip)— [where 'Julius' is again defined as in section 5.3].
   (d) (Necessarily) (the first mammal on the moon was human).
   (e) (Necessarily) (Neil Armstrong was human).
   (f) (The first mammal on the moon) (was necessarily human).

4. Which of the statements in question 3 are true and which false?

5. Which of these truths are necessary and which contingent?

   (a) Archie Leach = Cary Grant.
   (b) Cary Grant = Cary Grant.
   (c) David Papineau is a philosopher.
   (d) Julius [defined as before] invented the zip.
   (e) David Papineau's parents were Owen and Constance Papineau.
   (f) The parents of the oldest son of Owen and Constance Papineau were Owen and Constance Papineau.
   (g) Holland is The Netherlands.
   (h) Holland is the netherlands.

6. Which of the truths in question 5 are a priori and which a posteriori?

Part III

THE NATURE AND USES OF PROBABILITY

7

· • • • ·

Kinds of Probability

7.1 Probabilities of Propositions

Given any proposition p, then we can speak of the probability of p.

For example: the probability that the next card from this pack will be an ace, that this radium atom will decay before the year 3612, that Johnny will go to the party, that it will rain tomorrow, …

I shall write Pr(p) for the probability of p.

7.2 Kolmogorov's Axioms

In a moment I shall consider what it might mean to say that a certain proposition has a certain probability.

But before that we can note some basic arithmetical constraints. If a way of attaching numbers Pr(p) to propositions p is to count as an ascription of probabilities, it must at least observe the following requirements.

(1) For any p, $0 \leq Pr(p) \leq 1$

(2) If p is certain, $Pr(p) = 1$

(3) If p and q are incompatible, $P(p \text{ or } q) = Pr(p) + Pr(q)$

These are known as Kolmogorov's axioms, and were originally laid out by the great Russian mathematician Andrey Kolmogorov (1903–1987).

The axioms are simple enough. To illustrate, Pr(Johnny goes to the party) is a number between 0 and 1; if it is certain that Johnny will go to the party, then Pr(Johnny goes to the party) = 1; and if Johnny can't go both to the party and the football match, then Pr(Johnny goes to the party *or* the football march) = Pr(Johnny goes to the party) + Pr(Johnny goes to the football match).

7.3 Some Consequences

One immediate consequence of Kolmogorov's axioms is:

(4) $Pr(\text{not-}p) = 1 - Pr(p)$

To see why (4) follows from the axioms, note that p and not-p are incompatible, so by (3)

$P(p \text{ or not-}p) = Pr(p) + Pr(\text{not-}p)$.

But (p or not-p) is certain, so by (2)

$Pr(p \text{ or not-}p) = 1$.

The result follows by comparing the right-hand sides of these last two equations.

Here is another useful consequence. In general, whether or not p and q are incompatible:

(5) $Pr(p \text{ or } q) = Pr(p) + Pr(q) - Pr(p \text{ and } q)$.

Here 'p or q' should be understood as 'p and/or q', not as 'p or q but not both'. ('Or' will be understood in this sense throughout the book. Logicians call this the 'inclusive' sense, as opposed to the 'exclusive' sense of 'p or q but not both'.)

In this inclusive sense, it will be true that *Johnny goes to the party* or *wears a tie* if he does either on its own and also if he does both, by going to the party in a tie. And so understood Pr(Johnny goes to the party or wears a tie) = Pr(Johnny goes to the party) + Pr(Johnny wears a tie) − Pr(Johnny goes to the party *and* wears a tie).

It is possible to show that (5) follows from Kolmogorov's axioms, but the proof is somewhat laborious, so I shall leave it as an Exercise.

It is much easier to see why (5) must be true by inspecting a Venn diagram. When we look at the diagram, we see that simply adding Pr(p) to Pr(q) would count Pr(p and q) twice—so to get Pr(p or q) we need to correct by subtracting a Pr(p and q). (See Box 15.)

7.4 Joint Probabilities

The equivalence (5) told us that

$$Pr(p \text{ or } q) = Pr(p) + Pr(q) - Pr(p \text{ and } q).$$

However, there is no general rule for the size of Pr(p and q), nor therefore for how much we need to take away from the sum of Pr(p) and Pr(q) to get Pr(p or q). It depends on how much the Venn diagrams for p and q overlap with each other. In our example, it depends on how likely it is that Johnny will both go to the party *and* wear a tie.

We shall consider such joint probabilities—Pr(p and q)—in more detail in the next two chapters, when we discuss conditional probabilities and probabilistic independence. But we can usefully make some initial points here.

In some cases, Pr(p and q) will be zero, namely, when p and q are incompatible—their Venn diagrams don't overlap at all—and then Pr(p or q) will be the simple sum of Pr(p) and Pr(q), as in Kolmogorov's third axiom. This would be the case in our example if there is no way that Johnny would go to the party in a tie.

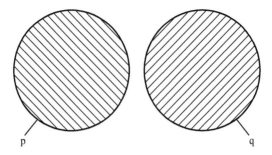

But in other cases p and q need not be incompatible, and then Pr(p and q) will be a positive number.

In the extreme case, p will entail q, or q entail p. (For example, Johnny's going to the party may *require* him to wear a tie.)

If p entails q, then the Venn diagram for p is *inside* that for q, so

Pr(p and q) = Pr(p)

and

Pr(p or q) = Pr(q).

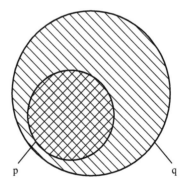

Box 15 Venn Diagrams

....

This 'Venn diagram' shows why Pr(p or q) = Pr(p) + Pr(q) − Pr(p and q).

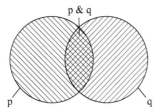

In a Venn diagram we take the points in a plane to represent possible worlds, and so can use sets of points to represent sets of possible worlds, and in particular to represent all those possible worlds where some proposition p is true. The areas of these spaces can then be used to represent the probabilities of the relevant propositions. (Note here how it is possible to equate a proposition with the set of possible worlds where it is true. This equivalence is widely used in philosophy.)

In the above diagram the proposition **p or q** corresponds to the points which are either in the area labelled p, or in the area labelled q, or in both. And the proposition **p and q** corresponds to the points which are in both the area labelled p *and* in the area labelled q—that is, the cross-hatched area.

It is easy to see that, if we tried to work out the area corresponding to **p or q** by simply adding the area for p to that for q, we would count the cross-hatched area twice. So to get the right answer we need to correct by subtracting the cross-hatched area.

In our example, if Johnny's going to the party requires him to wear a tie, then the Venn diagram for Johnny's going to the party will be inside the one for his wearing a tie, so

Pr(Johnny goes to the party *and* wears a tie) = Pr(Johnny goes to the party)

and therefore

Pr(Johnny goes to the party *or* wears a tie) = Pr(Johnny wears a tie).

If q entails p, then the Venn diagram for q is inside that for p, and these results are reversed.

So Pr(p and q) can sometimes equal Pr(p) and sometime equal Pr(q) (when p entails q or when q entails p respectively).

But note that Pr(p and q) can never *exceed* either of these numbers. Pr(Johnny goes to the party *and* wears a tie) can't be greater than either Pr(Johnny goes to the party) or Pr(Johnny wears a tie).

Sometimes it is easy to forget this. (See Box 16.) But you shouldn't. Two things both happening (p *and* q) can never be more likely than either one happening on its own.

7.5 Subjective and Objective Probabilities

There are two quite different ways of interpreting probability statements—that is, of understanding what it means when we attach numbers between 0 and 1 to propositions in such a way as to satisfy Kolmogorov's axioms of probability.

We can understand such statements either as reports about *subjective* probabilities or as reports about *objective* probabilities.

Subjective probabilities measure the extent to which *agents expect* outcomes. Objective probability measures the *real tendencies* for those outcomes to occur.

Box 16 Linda the Feminist Bank Teller

Let me tell you about Linda. She is 31 years old, single, outspoken, and very bright. She did an undergraduate degree in philosophy. As a student, she was deeply concerned with issues of discrimination and social justice, and also participated in anti-nuclear demonstrations.

Now, which of these propositions is more probable?

(A) Linda is a bank teller.

(B) Linda is a bank teller and is active in the feminist movement.

It is very natural to choose (B). When the psychologists Daniel Kahneman and Amos Tversky tested people on this question, they found that about 9 out of 10 chose (B). Indeed, when they tested doctoral students in the decision science programme at Stanford Business School, a group with an intensive training in probability and statistical theory, they still found that over 8 out of 10 chose (B).

Yet (B) cannot be the right answer. Two things cannot be more likely than one. After all, in every situation where Linda is a bank teller *and* a feminist, she will also be a bank teller; and in addition there will be situations where she is a bank teller without being a feminist.

Something about the Linda story confuses our thinking. (If you're not convinced that (B) is wrong, it might be helpful to think in terms of money. Suppose you are going to win £100 for a correct answer. Would you rather commit yourself to (A) or to (B)?)

7.6 Subjective Probability

Imagine that you are going out for a short walk, and you take both your sunglasses and your umbrella. Do you believe it is going to rain?

Well, you aren't certain it *is* going to rain—otherwise why take your sunglasses?

But you aren't certain that it is *not* going to rain either—otherwise why take your umbrella?

In a case like this, it seems natural to say that you have a certain *degree of belief* in the proposition *it will rain,* and that this can be represented by some number between 0 and 1. (If you were certain it will not rain, then your degree of belief would be 0, and if you were certain it will rain, then your degree of belief would be 1.)

Alternative names for these degrees of belief are 'subjective probabilities' or 'personal probabilities' or 'credences'.

7.7 Action, Utility, and Subjective Probability

We can think of degrees of belief as manifesting themselves in choices of actions (as when you took both your umbrella and your sunglasses in the example above). In general, the greater degree of belief an agent attaches to some proposition p, the more that agent will be inclined to perform actions that will bring good results *if* p.

The easiest way to connect degrees of belief with choice of actions is to focus on *betting* behaviour. Given some proposition p, ask yourself how much you would be prepared to pay for a bet that will pay £1 *if* p. (For example, how much are you prepared to pay to win £1 *if Johnny comes to the party?*) The fraction of £1 that you are prepared to stake plausibly measures your degree of belief in p. You'll be prepared to bet 50p if your degree of belief is 0.5, but only 10p if your degree of belief is 0.1.

Maybe you don't think of yourself as much of a gambler. But note that pretty much any action can be construed as a gamble. When you cross the road, this is presumably because your degree of belief that you will get to the other side (a good result) is very much bigger than your degree of belief that you will be run over (a very bad result).

Many philosophers and economists hold that, in general, when someone performs an action, this is because the *expected utility* of that action is greater than that of the alternative actions available. The idea here is that the agent is concerned about certain outcomes (getting to the other side, being run over) whose importance can be measured by some positive or negative number—its '*utility*'. And the *expected utility* of an action is then the sum of those utilities each multiplied by the agent's degree of belief that the action will lead to that outcome.

Thus suppose the utility of getting to the other side is plus 10, and your degree of belief that crossing the road will lead to this is 0.9999; and the utility of being run over is minus 10,000, and your degree of belief for this is 0.0001. Then the expected utility of crossing the road will be:

$$(10 \times 0.9999) + (-10,000 \times 0.0001) = 9.999 - 1 = 8.999$$

and this may well be higher than the expected utility of the alternative actions currently open to you.

Of course all this is at best a kind of idealization. In truth, there isn't really a precise answer to the question of exactly how much I believe p, for every proposition p. There are plenty of propositions that I have never thought of, and even among those I have thought of are many to which I have a pretty fuzzy attitude. Nor is it very realistic to suppose that I can attach numbers to all the things I care about. Still, perhaps we can go along with the idealization in order to simplify the arguments that follow. (Compare the way in which engineers simplify their calculations by assuming that everyday objects like a block of concrete have precise masses, even though in truth it will always be a bit vague whether some of the molecules on the surface are attached to the block or not.)

So I shall assume henceforth that for any person X, at any time t, and any proposition p, there will be a number between 0 and 1 that represents X's degrees of belief at time t in proposition p.

7.8 Dutch Books

I said that degrees of belief or subjective probabilities offer one way of interpreting probability statements—that is, one way of attaching numbers between 0 and 1 to propositions in such a way as to satisfy the axioms of probability.

However, as yet I haven't really shown this, for I haven't yet shown that degrees of belief do satisfy the axioms of probability.

And in fact there is no guarantee that they will. Nothing in psychology rules out the possibility that an agent at a time might attach a degree of belief 0.6 to the proposition *it will rain* and simultaneously a degree of belief 0.6 to the proposition *it won't rain*, thus violating the immediate implication of the probability axioms that Pr(p) = 1 − Pr(not-p). (Maybe the agent wasn't thinking very hard, and somehow managed to take a positive view of both these propositions at the same time.)

However, there is an argument that any *rational* degrees of belief must conform to the axioms of probability, even if *actual* degrees of belief don't always do so.

The argument is that anybody whose degrees of belief violate the axioms of probability can have a '*Dutch Book*' made against them. A Dutch Book is a set of bets which are *guaranteed to win whatever happens*.

By way of illustration, consider the person who believes *it will rain* to degree 0.6 and also believes *it won't rain* to degree 0.6. Well, this person will happily pay 60p to win £1 on its raining, and also happily pay 60p to win £1 on its *not* raining. But anybody who makes this pair of bets will certainly lose whatever happens, because they will have paid out £1.20 in total and will only win £1 whether it rains or not.

It is not hard to prove that a Dutch Book can be made against you if and only if your degrees of belief fail to satisfy the axioms of probability.

(The subject in the above illustration got into trouble because of degrees of belief in p and not-p which added to more than 1. This might make it seem safe to have degrees of belief that add to *less* than 1. However, in that case you could be induced to bet *against* both p and not-p in a way that is guaranteed to lose.)

Since it seems clearly irrational to adopt attitudes that can make it certain that you will incur a loss, it follows that any rational agent will have degrees of belief that do conform to the probability calculus. (Such agents are called 'coherent'; those whose degrees of belief violate the axioms are 'incoherent'.) (See Box 17.)

Note that there is nothing in this 'Dutch Book Argument' to specify *what* degrees of belief you should have, beyond requiring that they must conform to the probability axioms. You can be coherent by having a subjective probability of 0.6 for *it will rain* and of 0.4 for *it won't rain*. But you could equally achieve coherence by attaching 0.8 and 0.2 to these two propositions, or 0.15 and 0.85, or any other combination of numbers that add up to 1.

The 'Dutch Book Argument' requires coherence, but beyond that leaves it to subjective opinion which particular degrees of belief you should adopt.

7.9 Objective Probability

Objective probabilities are quite different from subjective ones. They are out in the world, not in people's heads. They quantify the objective tendencies for certain kinds of results to happen. These tendencies would still have existed even if agents with subjective probabilities had never evolved.

The clearest examples of objective probabilities come from the quantum mechanics of subatomic processes. Certain events at this level are absolutely unpredictable. Take any radium atom. It may decay in a given time interval or it may not. There is no difference between those atoms that decay and those that don't. All that can be said is that each such atom has a certain objective probability of decaying in a given interval. (If the interval is 1602 years—the 'half-life' of a radium atom—then there is 0.5 probability of decay in that time.)

It is helpful to think of objective probabilities in terms of *frequencies*. If the probability of a single radium atom decaying within its half-life is 0.5, then about 50% of any sequence of radium atoms will decay in that time.

(But don't be too quick to *equate* objective probabilities with frequencies. There are many philosophical pitfalls in the way of any such equation, most centrally the fact that the observed frequency in any sequence of events won't generally correspond *exactly* to the underlying probability. Note how I was careful to say above that '*about* 50% of any sequence of radium atoms will decay in that time'—not that exactly 50% will.)

There are plenty of objective probabilities outside the subatomic world (though perhaps they all depend in some way on quantum probabilities). For example, the probability that any human embryo will be male is slightly over 0.5. The probability that males in the United States will develop pancreatic cancer in their lifetime is 0.0138. The probability that an ace will be dealt first from a well-shuffled pack is 1/13. And so on.

The ultimate nature of objective probability is a matter of philosophical controversy. But we need not enter into this here. The basic point is that objective probabilities are genuine features of the external world, distinct from subjective degrees of belief.

Box 17 Bookmakers and Dutch Books

A good bookmaker aims to make a Dutch Book against the punters. The bookie wants to induce the punters to make a set of bets that will turn a profit for the bookie whichever horse wins.

For instance, in a two-horse race between Aramis and Balthazar, the bookie will be guaranteed a profit whichever horse wins if £100 has been staked on Aramis at evens, and £120 on Balthazar at 2-1 on. ('Evens' means that you stake £1 to win £1, and '2-1 on' means you stake £2 to win £1.) These bets mean that the bookie will make £20 if Aramis wins (the £120 stake on Balthzar less the £100 payout on Aramis) and £40 if Balthazar wins (the £100 stake on Aramis less the £60 paid out on Balthazar).

This doesn't necessarily mean that any individual punter is irrational. The bookie can pull this trick because different punters will sometimes attach different subjective probabilities to the same outcome. In this sense the punters *taken collectively* will violate the axioms of probability. But this doesn't mean that any individual punter has 'incoherent' degrees of belief.

But you will be irrational if the bookie can make a Dutch Book against you all *on your own*. If you yourself put £100 on Aramis at evens, and *also* put £120 on Balthasar at 2-1 on, then this indicates that you personally have a degree of belief in Aramis winning of at least 1/2 and in Aramis *not* winning of at least 2/3. Now the bookie is not only sure to win, but you individually are sure to lose.

FURTHER READING

Two of my old teachers have written excellent philosophical introductions to probability:

An Introduction to Probability and Inductive Logic by Ian Hacking (Cambridge University Press 2001).

Probability: A Philosophical Introduction by D. H. Mellor (Routledge 2005).

The Stanford Encyclopedia entry by Alan Hayek is a thorough discussion of the different 'interpretations of probability': <http://plato.stanford.edu/entries/probability-interpret>.

Daniel Kahneman's *Thinking, Fast and Slow* (Allen Lane 2011) explains how humans are very prone to mistakes in probabilistic reasoning.

EXERCISES

1. If I draw one card from a well-shuffled pack, what is the probability of:

   (a) a heart
   (b) a king
   (c) an honour (A, K, Q, J, 10)
   (d) not a heart
   (e) an honour and a heart
   (f) a heart or a spade
   (g) a heart and a spade?

2. If I toss a fair coin four times, what is the probability that I get:

   (a) four heads; (b) zero heads; (c) one head; (d) three heads?

   Hint: there are 16 equiprobable outcomes for the four-toss sequence.

3. If I roll two fair dice, what is the probability that they sum to:

   (a) 4; (b) 7; (c) 12; (d) an odd number; (e) less than 5; (f) either less than 5 or 9; (g) either less than 5 or an even number?

   Hint: there are 36 equiprobable ways the dice can land.

4. If Pr(Johnny at party) = 0.4 and Pr(Jenny at party) = 0.8 and Pr(Johnny and Jenny at party) = 0.3, what is the probability that

   (a) Jenny won't be there
   (b) at least one of them will be there
   (c) Jenny will be there but not Johnny?

5. Suppose that you can either go to the beach or to watch the test match. The beach has an intrinsic utility of plus 10, and the cricket of plus 15. But there is a 0.5 chance that you will get sunburnt (utility of minus 10) at the beach, where there is only a 0.3 chance of getting sunburnt at the cricket. Also, there is a 0.2 chance you will see Jill (plus 20) at the beach, but only a 0.05 chance you will see her at the cricket. Which option has the greater expected utility?

6*. Show algebraically how the equation

$$Pr(p \text{ or } q) = Pr(p) + Pr(q) - Pr(p \text{ and } q)$$

follows from Kolmogorov's axioms. (Hint: note that

$(p \text{ or } q)$ is logically equivalent to $((p \And \text{not-}q) \text{ or } (q))$

and that

p is logically equivalent $((p \And q) \text{ or } (p \And \text{not-}q))$

and that the pairs of propositions within the brackets on the right-hand sides are incompatible.)

8

· · • · ·

Constraints on Credence

8.1 The Principal Principle

The last chapter ended with the contrast between subjective and objective probabilities. Some readers might have wondered how they are related.

Not every proposition to which agents attach subjective degrees of belief will also have an objective probability. You might well have a certain expectation of Johnny going to the party, say, or of Aramis winning the 3.30 at Kempton Park, even if there is no good sense in which these propositions have any objective probability.

But in other cases agents do attach subjective degrees of belief to propositions that also have an objective probability—for example, that a given atom will decay in some interval, or that a given embryo will be male, or that the next card drawn from a well-shuffled pack will be a spade.

Now, there is no guarantee in such cases that the agent's subjective probability will correspond to the objective probability. You might *expect* a spade to degree 1/2, even though its objective probability is only 1/4.

But even so there is something obvious to say about the relation between subjective and objective probability in such cases—namely

The Principal Principle:
An agent's subjective probabilities *ought* to match the objective probabilities, even if in fact they don't.

The term 'Principal Principle' was originally coined by David Lewis (the same philosopher who was a realist about possible worlds) for his version of the idea that subjective probabilities ought to match objective probabilities. He adopted this name because he thought that this idea is fundamental to our understanding of both objective and subjective probability.

In fact my Principal Principle above is only a rough approximation to Lewis' more carefully formulated principle. But it will do for present purposes.

Remember that the 'Dutch Book Argument' allowed rational agents a great deal of freedom about the choice of subjective probabilities—the only constraint was that subjective probabilities should conform to the axioms of probability. The Principal Principle imposes a further constraint on rational agents—when objective probabilities exist, you should do what you can to make your subjective probabilities match them.

The Principal Principle is obviously sensible. If you are to make the right choices, your subjective expectations had better not diverge from the objective probabilities. You will make bad bets if you have a high degree of belief that a spade will be dealt, when in fact the objective probability is only 1/4.

Curiously, even though conformity to the Principal Principle is obviously a good idea, the status of this principle is a matter of controversy. Some philosophers think it can be justified by appeal to more basic facts. But others doubt that any such justification is possible, and view it as itself a fundamental principle of rationality.

8.2 Conditional Probability

The *conditional probability* of p given q, Pr(p/q), is the probability to ascribe to p on the assumption that q.

It is measured by:

(1) Pr(p/q) = Pr(p & q)/Pr(q).

(In Venn diagram terms, think: the area of q that is also p—that is, the cross-hatched area as a proportion of the area for q.)

So, for example, we might have the conditional probability that a throw of a fair die will show an even number, given that it shows a higher number than three. We can write this Pr(even/over three), and measure it by:

Pr(even *and* over three)/ Pr(over three).

This fraction represents the probability of an even result among the results that are higher than three—and is equal to 2/3, since the probability of a result (four or six) that is even *and* over three is 2/6, while the probability of *any* result over three (four, five, or six) is 1/2.

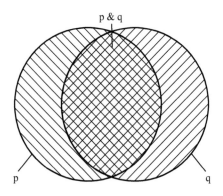

8.3 Updating Degrees of Belief—Conditionalization

Now that we have introduced conditional probabilities, we can explain a further constraint governing rational degrees of belief. So far we have seen how the 'Dutch Book Argument' implies that rational degrees of belief must be *coherent* (that is, satisfy the axioms of probability), and how the Principal Principle implies that they must *match objective probabilities* when these are available. The further constraint is that rational agents should '*conditionalize*' whenever they gain new information.

Suppose that you have rational degrees of belief as follows:

Pr(Johnny goes to the party) = 1/2
Pr(Johnny goes to the party/Jane goes to the party) = 2/3.

Now you learn for sure that Jane is going to the party. What should your degree of belief in Johnny's going now be?

The answer is obvious enough—2/3. If it was right to think beforehand that the conditional probability of *Johnny going/on the assumption Jane goes* is 2/3, and if now it turns out that Jane *is* going, then it must be

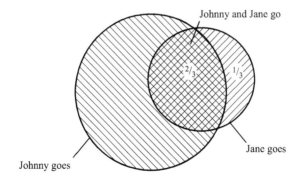

right to think that the unconditional probability of Johnny has increased to 2/3.

Think of it in Venn diagram terms. You now know you are *inside* the area of the Venn diagram for Jane's going, so to speak. And you have already decided that the proportion of this area that covers Johnny going is 2/3. So it must now be rational for you to have an unconditional degree of belief in Johnny going of 2/3.

Changing your degrees of belief in this way is called '*conditionalization*'. Let us thus formulate

The Principle of Conditionalization:
If your *old* conditional degree of belief $Pr_{old}(p/q)$ equals k, and you come to know q, you should set your *new* degree of belief in p, $Pr_{new}(p)$, equal to k.

Note that q here needs to be understood as representing *everything* you come to know. The principle doesn't work if q is only *part* of your new knowledge.

Thus suppose that in the above example you learn not only that Jane is going to the party but also that she will be accompanied by Jill. And suppose that you had always thought that there was almost no chance that Johnny would go if *both* Jane and Jill did. (You had a very low original conditional probability Pr_{old}(Johnny goes/Jane *and* Jill go) even though your original Pr_{old}(Johnny goes/Jane goes) was 2/3.)

While it is still true that you have learned that *Jane will go*, it is no longer a good idea to attach a 2/3 probability to Johnny going, just on the grounds that your Pr_{old}(Johnny goes/Jane goes) = 2/3. And this is precisely because you have learned *more* than that Jane will go to the party. You now know not just that you are inside Jane's Venn diagram, so to speak, but more specifically that you are inside that bit of it where Jill also goes to the party. And the proportion of *that* area where Johnny goes too is very small.

It is generally agreed *that* the Principle of Conditionalization is valid. But, just as with the Principal Principle, there is no agreement about *why* it is valid. As before, some philosophers think it is a basic principle of rationality, while others think that it can be justified by further considerations.

Note in this connection that the Principle of Conditionalization is *not* simply a consequence of the Dutch Book Argument for coherence. That earlier argument showed that the axioms of probability must be respected by all the degrees of belief you adopt *at any given time*. But the Principle of Conditionalization concerns the way you should *change* your degrees of belief *over time* in response to evidence, substituting your old degrees of belief $Pr_{old}(\text{---})$ by new ones $Pr_{new}(\text{---})$.

You will satisfy the Dutch Book Argument as long as your old $Pr_{old}(\text{---})$s and your new $Pr_{new}(\text{---})$s are each separately coherent. The Principle of Conditionalization places a further constraint on the how these two sets of degrees of belief are related.

8.4 Bayes' Theorem

There is a simple probability equation that casts some useful light on the workings of conditionalization:

(2) $Pr(h/e) = Pr(h) \times Pr(e/h)/Pr(e)$.

This equation, which you can check follows very quickly from the equation (1) for conditional probability, is known as *Bayes' Theorem*, after the eighteenth-century English clergyman who first proved it.

To see the significance of this equation, consider some case where you gain some evidence e and are concerned with its bearing on some hypothesis h. According to the Principle of Conditionalization, you should adopt a new $Pr_{new}(h)$ that is equal to your old conditional $Pr_{old}(h/e)$. But Bayes' Theorem tells us that $Pr_{old}(h/e)$ is equal to $Pr_{old}(h) \times Pr_{old}(e/h)/Pr_{old}(e)$. So we can see that the two together imply that

(3) $Pr_{new}(h) = Pr_{old}(h) \times Pr_{old}(e/h)/Pr_{old}(e)$.

We can view this as a recipe for transforming your old degree of belief in h to a new one when your learn e—multiply your $Pr_{old}(h)$ by the factor on the right-hand side. This tells you that you should increase your degree of belief in h to just the extent that $Pr_{old}(e/h)$ exceeded $Pr_{old}(e)$—that is, to just the extent that e was to be expected given h but not to be expected otherwise.

So viewed, (3) seems eminently sensible. The hypothesis h is confirmed if it successfully predicts something that would otherwise be unexpected.

In addition to thus explaining why a hypothesis gains more credibility from the verification of *surprising* rather than unsurprising consequences, Bayes' Theorem also illuminates a wide range of other quirks and puzzles about the way evidence confirms hypotheses.

For example, (3) explains why it is a mistake to ignore the prior probability of h in assessing how probable it is shown to be by e. (This surprisingly common mistake is known as the 'base rate fallacy'. See Box 18.)

Because of the significance of Bayes' theorem, the term '*Bayesian*' is often found in discussions of probability. However, this term has no very definite meaning. It is probably most often used to refer to any view that takes subjective degrees of belief seriously and holds that they are subject to some rational principles. But sometimes it is used more precisely, to refer specifically to the idea that degrees of belief should be updated according to the Principle of Conditionalization.

8.5 Conditional Probabilities and Conditional Statements

A conditional probability $Pr(q/p)$ is the probability of q *on the assumption that* p.

Some readers might have wondered how such conditional probabilities relate to *conditional statements* of the form *if p, then q*. (For example: *if Jane goes to the party, then Johnny will go too.*)

After all, doesn't a conditional statement amount to something like stating q *on the assumption* that p? And given this, shouldn't we expect the probability of the conditional statement Pr(if p, then q) to be equal to the conditional probability Pr(q/p)?

As it happens, this is a horribly complicated topic.

An initial difficulty is that there are different kinds of conditional statement. In a moment I shall distinguish between *material*, *indicative*, and *subjunctive* conditionals. And even after we have distinguished them, it is not obvious how to understand them. While material conditionals are clear enough, the analysis of indicative and subjunctive conditionals is hugely controversial.

It would take us too far afield to analyse these constructions properly here. My aim in the brief remainder of this chapter will simply be to show you why we need to recognize different kinds of conditionals.

What about the question with which I started this section—is the probability of a conditional statement Pr(if p, then q) equal to the conditional probability Pr(q/p)? Here I can do no more than simply tell you that this simple equation doesn't work for *any* kind of conditional 'if..., then' statement—which is not to deny that there are important connections between conditional statements and conditional probabilities.

8.6 Material Conditionals

If you have done an elementary logic course, you will have been introduced to a construction, normally written 'p→q', which is defined as being true as long as it is not the case that p is true and q is false.

This is the 'material conditional'.

Given its definition, it is easy to see that 'p→q' is equivalent to 'not-(p and not-q)' or again to 'either not-p or q'.

It is normal in elementary logic courses to read 'p→q' as 'if p, then q'.

And indeed the material conditional does have strong similarities with everyday claims of the form 'if p, then q'. In particular, it shares the feature that, when you add knowledge of p to them, then you can infer q. Just as p together with 'if p, then q' implies q, so does p together with 'p→q'. (This is an immediate consequence of the definition of 'p→q' given above—you can check it as an exercise.)

Given the similarities, there is no great harm in reading 'p→q' as equivalent to everyday claims of the form 'if p, then q' when exploring elementary logic. But there are strong reasons to doubt that the two constructions are really the same.

Note that 'p→q' is guaranteed to be true whenever p is false, whatever q says, and also to be true whenever q is true, whatever p says. (Remember, 'p→q' is true as long as it is not both the case that p is true and q is false.)

So 'David Papineau goes to Antigua in November → the gold price rises in December' is guaranteed to be true, as long as I do not go to Antigua in November.

Similarly 'Cesc Fabregas plays for Arsenal → Hugh Grant lives in London' is guaranteed to be true, simply in virtue of Hugh Grant living in London.

Now, as we shall see in a moment, the everyday construction 'if…, then…' can be used to make two different kinds of claim—'indicative' and 'subjunctive' conditional claims. But we can already see reasons why the material conditional 'p→q' must differ from both of these. In ordinary English, any claim of the form 'if p, then q' requires some *connection* between p and q, not just the falsity of the antecedent p or the truth of the consequent q.

So, on any reading of the English construction 'if…, then…', my not going to Antigua in November isn't enough to ensure the truth of '*if* David Papineau goes to Antigua in November, *then* the gold price will rise in December'—for there may be no connection between my November location and the December gold price.

Box 18 The Base Rate Fallacy

....

You are worried about a kind of cancer (h) which is present in 1% of people like you. There is a simple test which invariably detects the cancer, though it does give a false positive result in 10% of people without it. You take the test, and get a positive result (e). What now is the probability you have the cancer?

Well, you might think that, since the test is only 10% unreliable, the answer must be 90%. But that would be quite wrong. There is still little more than a 9% probability of cancer.

To see why, recall that, once you discover e, you should set your new $Pr_{new}(h)$ equal to your old $Pr_{old}(h/e)$. And Bayes' Theorem tells you to compute this by multiplying your old $Pr_{old}(h)$ by $Pr_{old}(e/h)/Pr_{old}(e)$.

Two of these terms are easy. $Pr_{old}(h)$ was given as 1%, and $Pr_{old}(e/h)$ is 1, since the test invariably detects the cancer. $Pr_{old}(e)$ is a bit messier: what is the probability of a positive result for a person taken at random? Well, the 1% of cancer sufferers will definitely give positive results, and the 99% of non-sufferers will give 10% false positives—which sums to 10.9%. So $Pr_{old}(h) \times Pr_{old}(e/h)/Pr_{old}(e) = 0.01 \times 1/0.109 \approx 0.0917$. So you should set your $Pr_{new}(h)$ to just over 9%.

Think of it like this. If 1,000 people take the test, 10 will give a positive result because they have the cancer—but 99 healthy people will give false positives. So a bad result still leaves you with only a $10/109 \approx 0.0917$ probability of cancer.

The tendency to overestimate the significance of such tests is called the 'base rate fallacy', because it is due to ignoring the low 'base rate' or initial probability of having the cancer. It is disturbingly common in everyday life.

And similarly Hugh Grant's living in London isn't enough to ensure the truth of '*if* Cesc Fabregas plays for Arsenal, *then* Hugh Grant lives in London'—for Cesc Fabregas' employment may have nothing to do with Hugh Grant's residence.

Given these differences, it seems clear that the material conditional works differently from any version of the everyday construction 'if p, then q'. (Indeed, we might feel that 'material *conditional*' is something of a misnomer, given its marked difference from any everyday 'if p, then q'.)[1]

8.7 Indicative and Subjunctive Conditionals

Consider this pair of claims.

(4) 'If Oswald didn't kill Kennedy, then someone else did.'

This claim is obviously true. There is no doubt that President Kennedy was killed by somebody. If Lee Harvey Oswald wasn't in fact the guilty party, then some else must have done it.

(5) 'If Oswald hadn't killed Kennedy, then someone else would have.'

This claim is very doubtful. The Warren Commission investigated the matter very thoroughly and concluded that Oswald was working alone. In their view, if Oswald's plans had somehow been frustrated, then Kennedy would not have been killed—that is, they concluded that (5) is false.

Since (4) is clearly true and (5) very likely false, they must mean different things.

---

[1] I should note that there are a few philosophers who maintain that the indicative version of the everyday 'if p, then q' is at bottom no different from the material conditional, and that the apparent discrepancies can be explained away. But this is very much a minority position.

THE NATURE AND USES OF PROBABILITY

But note that *both* claims are of the form 'if p, then q' and both have the *same* antecedent p—Oswald not killing Kennedy—and the *same* consequent q—someone else killing Kennedy.

The only difference between the two claims is that (4) is in the *indicative* mood ('… didn't kill … did.') while (5) is in the *subjunctive* mood ('… hadn't killed … would have').

Accordingly, claims like (4) are called indicative conditionals and claims like (5) subjunctive conditionals.

(Sometimes subjunctive conditionals are called 'counterfactual' on the grounds that they imply the falsity of their antecedents. But this terminology can be misleading, given that plenty of indicative conditionals also have antecedents that are pretty sure to be false—(4) would be a case in point.)

8.8 Rational and Metaphysical Changes

Let me say a bit more about the difference between indicative and subjunctive conditionals. (I can only scratch the surface here. The analysis of these constructions is hugely controversial, with a literature stretching to thousands and thousands of articles. There are philosophers who spend their whole lives working on conditionals—indeed there are philosophers who work only on indicative conditionals, and others who work only on subjunctive conditionals.)

Indicative conditionals are to do with rational changes of belief. They tell us what we should believe on learning the antecedent p.

Subjunctive conditionals are to do with metaphysical alternatives. They tell us what difference p would have made to the course of history.

To illustrate how indicative conditionals work, suppose that someone whom you trust whispers in your ear that Lee Harvey Oswald definitely didn't kill President Kennedy. What should you now think?

Well, you know full well that Kennedy was assassinated, and your new information doesn't contradict this. So the obvious conclusion is that there was a different assassin. Thus: 'If Oswald didn't kill Kennedy, then someone else did.'

Now take the corresponding subjunctive conditional. The question now is the difference it would have made to history had Oswald not killed Kennedy, not how such information should impact on your beliefs. And to this question the obvious answer (assuming the Warren Commission was right) is that Kennedy would not have been assassinated. Thus: 'If Oswald hadn't killed Kennedy, then no one else would have.'

When we evaluate indicative conditionals, we add p to *all* our current beliefs, make the minimum adjustments needed to accommodate it, and consider whether q still follows.

But when we evaluate subjunctive conditionals, we proceed differently. We first remove from our current beliefs all those whose truth is a causal consequence of not-p—and only then do we add p with minimal adjustments and consider whether q follows. Since we are concerned with the impact p would have on the course of history, we don't want to reason on the basis of facts that would have been causally altered if p had obtained.

That's why we don't hold onto Kennedy's assassination when we make the *subjunctive* assumption 'if Oswald hadn't killed Kennedy …'. Removing Oswald's killing Kennedy removes the cause of Kennedy's assassination.

By contrast, we *do* hold onto Kennedy's assassination when we make the *indicative* assumption 'if Oswald didn't kill Kennedy…'. Since we are sure that Kennedy actually was killed, we hang onto this information in evaluating the indicative conditional.

FURTHER READING

Colin Howson and Peter Urbach's *Scientific Reasoning: The Bayesian Approach* (Open Court second edition 1993) shows how 'Bayesianism' illuminates many aspects of scientific reasoning.

Paul Horwich's *Probability and Evidence* (Cambridge University Press 1982) covers much of the same ground.

There is a useful Stanford Encyclopedia entry on Bayesian thinking by William Talbott: <http://plato.stanford.edu/entries/epistemology-bayesian>.

A *Philosophical Guide to Conditionals* (Oxford University Press 2003) by Jonathan Bennett is a masterly introduction to this complex topic.

Mark Sainsbury's *Logical Forms* (Blackwell second edition 2001) contains much useful material about conditionals and their connection with probabilities.

See also <http://plato.stanford.edu/entries/conditionals> by Dorothy Edgington.

EXERCISES

1. If Pr(wind) = 0.6, Pr(rain) = 0.5, and Pr(wind and rain) = 0.4, what is Pr(wind/rain), and what is Pr(rain/wind)?

2. If I draw one card from a well-shuffled pack, what is the conditional probability of:

   (a) a court cart (A, K, Q, J) given a heart
   (b) a court card given not a heart
   (c) a heart given a court card
   (d) not a heart given a court card
   (e) an even number given a non-court card
   (f) an odd number given a non-court card
   (g) an even number given a court card?

3. Suppose you have good reason to hold that Pr(h) = 0.1, Pr(e) = 0.2, and Pr(e/h) is 0.8. Then you learn e. What probability should you now attach to h?

4. You have a 10% degree of belief that a coin is not fair but has a 75% bias in favour of Heads. You toss it twice and see two Heads. What now should be your degree of belief that it is not fair?

5. Which of these conditionals are indicative and which subjunctive?

   (a) If you have visited the moon, then you have forgotten being there.
   (b) If you had visited the moon, then you would have forgotten being there.
   (c) If the British Prime Minister in 2012 were a woman, she would be in disguise.
   (d) If the British Prime Minister in 2012 is a woman, she is in disguise.
   (e) If you have eaten arsenic, then you are dead now.
   (f) If you had eaten arsenic, then you would be dead now.
   (g) If the foundations of Buckingham Palace had crumbled to dust, this wouldn't have made it collapse.
   (h) If the foundations of Buckingham Palace have crumbled to dust, this hasn't made it collapse.

6. Which of the conditionals in the last question are true, and which false?

9

. . • . .

Correlations and Causes

9.1 Probabilistic Independence

We say that p is *probabilistically independent* of q when Pr(p/q) = Pr(p).

In such a case, the probability of p on the assumption that q is no different from the probability of p in general. Assuming q doesn't alter the probability of p.

To illustrate, take the propositions that a card drawn from a pack will be an *honour* (10, Jack, Queen, King, or Ace) and that it will be a *heart*. The former is probabilistically independent of the latter. An honour is no more nor less likely on the assumption that the card is a heart than it is anyway.

Let us check the arithmetic. Pr(honour/heart) is Pr(honour *and* heart)—which is 5/52—divided by Pr(heart)—which is 1/4. So Pr(honour/heart) is 5/13, which is just the same as Pr(honour) itself. As I said, getting a heart doesn't make it any more or less likely that you will get an honour.

Note that p is probabilistically independent of q if and only if

(1) Pr(p and q) = Pr(p)Pr(q).

(To see why, remember that

$Pr(p/q) = Pr(p \text{ and } q)/Pr(q)$.

So, if

$Pr(p/q) = Pr(p)$ (that is, p is probabilistically independent of q)

then

$Pr(p \text{ and } q) = Pr(p)Pr(q)$,

and vice versa.)

Probabilistic independence thus means that p and q don't occur together any more (or less) often than you would expect given their separate probabilities of occurrence.

We also now see that probabilistic independence is symmetrical. If p is probabilistically independent of q, then q is probabilistically independent of p.

In our example, we have already seen that getting an honour is probabilistically independent of getting a heart. The probability of an honour isn't altered by getting a heart—it's 5/13 either way.

So by the same coin, getting a heart must be independent of getting an honour—and if you think for a second you'll see that the probability of a heart is indeed not altered by getting an honour—it's 1/4 either way.

Just as getting a heart doesn't make it any more or less likely that you will get an honour, so getting an honour doesn't make it any more or less likely that you will get a heart.

We see that when two results are independent, neither gives any information about the other.

9.2 Probabilistic Dependence

When $Pr(p \text{ and } q) > Pr(p)Pr(q)$, then we say p and q are *positively probabilistically dependent*.

This is equivalent to the requirements that

Pr(p/q) > Pr(p)

or that

Pr(q/p) > Pr(q).

In such cases q makes p more likely than it would be otherwise, and p makes q more likely than it would be otherwise.

So for example, getting an honour and getting a 9-or-a-10 are positively probabilistically dependent. The probability of having both (by getting a 10) is 1/13, which is greater than the product of the probabilities of getting an honour (5/13) and getting a 9-or-10 (2/13).

When Pr(p and q) < Pr(p)Pr(q)—equivalently Pr(p/q) < Pr(p) or Pr(q/p) < Pr(q)—then we say p and q are *negatively probabilistically dependent*.

Getting an honour and getting an even numbered card (2, 4, 6, 8, or 10) are negatively probabilistically dependent. The probability of getting both these results (you need a 10 again) is 1/13—which is *less* than the product of the probabilities of getting an honour (5/13) and getting an even-numbered card (1/2).

9.3 Correlation

We speak of correlations when we study the objective probabilistic dependencies between distinct properties of individuals. The individuals might be people, places, countries, cars, stars, cows,… pretty much anything whatever. If we were studying people, our properties might be gender, alcohol consumption, and heart disease, say. If we were studying cows, our properties might be diet, breed, weight, and fertility. And so on.

Suppose we represent the properties of interest in some such case as F, G, H,… We can then use Pr(F), Pr(G), Pr(H),…to represent the objective probability that any given individual will have property F, G, H,…respectively.

If in such a case F and G are positively probabilistically dependent—$Pr(F/G) > Pr(F)$—then we can say that F and G are *correlated*.

A correlation between F and G thus means that F occurs more often in the presence of G than otherwise (and vice versa). For example, we might find that in people heart disease (H) and drinking alcohol (A) are correlated—$Pr(H/A) > Pr(H)$. This tells us that the probability of heart disease among the alcohol drinkers is higher than in the population in general.[1]

9.4 Causation and Correlation

We're often told that correlation doesn't prove causation. And that's true enough—a craving for ice cream is correlated among women with giving birth some months later, but the craving doesn't cause the birth.

In this case, the correlation isn't due to the craving causing the birth, or vice versa, but to the presence of a common cause for both events—namely, pregnancy. The craving is thus a *symptom* of the impending birth, but not its cause.

Still, even if correlation doesn't always mean causation, because of the possibility of common causes, it is arguable that correlation between two properties does mean that *either* one causes another *or* they have a common cause.

To have a correlation without any such causal explanation would be an absurd general coincidence. Once-off coincidences are only to be

---

[1] Statistic textbooks will normally give a more complicated definition of correlation, to deal with quantitative properties like weight as well as on-off qualitative properties like gender. But we can ignore quantitative properties here, since they do not affect the basic philosophical points.

expected. Sometimes Jill and Jane will happen to find themselves wearing the same colour dress just by chance. But if this turns out to be a regular pattern, then it calls for explanation. (Either Jill is copying Jane, or Jane is copying Jill, or they are both influenced by the same fashion advice.)

If we accept that a correlation between two properties does indeed imply that either one is causing the other or that they have a common cause, then we can use this to help us infer causation from correlation. In particular, if we can rule out the possibility of a common cause, then we *can* infer a direct causal connection.

9.5 Screening Off

Interestingly, common causes have a distinctive probabilistic profile. They typically '*screen off*' the correlation between their joint effects, in the sense that this correlation disappears when we '*control for the common cause*'. This allows us to identify common causes from probabilistic patterns, and thereby tell whether or not correlations signify causal connections.

Let me explain this more slowly. Take the craving–birth correlation again. 'Controlling for the common cause' means looking separately

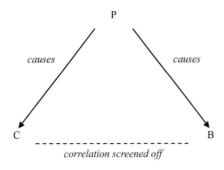

at cases where women are pregnant and where they are not. And, when we do this, the 'correlation disappears' in the sense that, in cases where women are pregnant, the craving for ice cream doesn't now make a subsequent birth any *more* likely, and similarly in cases where women are *not* pregnant. Once we take pregnancy into account, the craving can be seen to make no further difference to the probability of a birth. In this sense, pregnancy '*screens off*' the correlation between cravings and births.

In symbols, there is an initial correlation between craving (C) and birth (B)

$$Pr(B/C) > Pr(B)$$

but this correlation, represented by the dotted line in Diagram 12, is 'screened off' by pregnancy (P) in the sense that:

$$Pr(B/C \text{ and } P) = Pr(B/P)$$

and

$$Pr(B/C \text{ and not-P}) = Pr(B/\text{not-P}).$$

Once we know that the craving–birth correlation is 'screened off' by the prior pregnancy in this way, we can infer that there is no causal link between them, and that they are joint effects of pregnancy.

9.6 Spurious Correlations

Of course, we didn't *need* the probabilistic data from the last section to tell us that cravings for ice cream don't cause births. This knowledge is already part of common sense. But in other cases it is precisely such probabilistic data that enable us to find out what is causing what.

To go back to our earlier example, suppose we find that there is a correlation between heart disease (H) and alcohol consumption (A).

$$Pr(H/A) > Pr(H)$$

This might make us think that alcohol consumption causes heart disease. But now suppose that it turns out that gender screens off this correlation—the correlation disappears when we look separately at females (F) and males (not-F).

$$Pr(H/A \text{ and } F) = Pr(H/F)$$

and

$$Pr(H/A \text{ and } \text{not-F}) = Pr(H/\text{not-F}).$$

This would show that the initial correlation was misleading. Alcohol consumption turns out not to be a genuine cause of heart disease. The two properties are only correlated because gender is a common cause of both. Heart disease tends to be found with alcohol consumption only because being male conduces both to heart disease and to alcohol consumption. (Note that this is just an illustration—I make no claims about its medical accuracy.)

In such a case the original correlation is said to be '*spurious*'. This doesn't mean it is not a real correlation. It is—it is still true that heart disease is more common among the drinkers. But the correlation is spurious in that it doesn't correspond to any direct causal connection—rather the two correlated properties are joint effects of a common cause.

In cases of spurious correlation the common cause is often referred to as a 'confounding' property.

9.7 Randomized Experiments

If we find that some initial correlation between F and G is screened off by some earlier confounding property E, then we can be confident that F and G do not influence each other, but are joint effects of the common cause E, as in the pregnancy and heart disease examples just considered.

However, if we find that some particular earlier E does *not* screen off a correlation between F and G, then we can't immediately infer that G *does* cause F, or vice versa. For there may yet be other common causes we haven't yet identified.

For example, suppose that the heart disease/alcohol consumption correlation turned out *not* to be screened off by gender. We couldn't immediately conclude that alcohol *is* a cause of heart disease. For it may yet be that they are both joint effects of some other 'confounding' property, such as income level, or stress, or anything else—and then drinking would again only be a symptom of this underlying cause, and not itself responsible for heart disease.

The hard way to show that alcohol really is a cause of heart disease is to survey the population and check all the confounding properties that could possibly be responsible for a spurious correlation and show that none of them screens off the association.

But there is an easier way to show that one property is really a cause of another. Suppose we are able to perform a *'randomized experiment'*. The idea here is not to look at correlations in the population at large, but rather to pick out a sample of individuals, and arrange randomly for some to have the putative cause and some not.

The point of such a randomized experiment is to ensure that any correlation between the putative cause and effect *does* indicate a causal connection. This works because the randomization ensures that the putative cause is no longer itself systematically correlated with *any* other properties that exert a causal influence on the putative effect (such as gender, or income level, or stress,…, or *anything* else). So a remaining correlation between the putative cause and effect must mean that they really are causally connected.

So, for example, we might take a sample of people, and constrain some of them picked at random to drink alcohol and the rest to abstain, in the interests of finding out whether the former group develops more heart disease. Now, of course in this particular case there are obvious practical and ethical barriers to such an experiment. But in other cases it will be feasible.

Thus suppose we want to make sure that the correlation between some medical treatment and recovery from the relevant disease isn't just a spurious result of the treatment being available only to more affluent sufferers, say, or to some other confounding property. The standard solution is to perform a *randomized clinical trial* by taking a group of sufferers and giving the treatment only to a subgroup chosen at random. Many medical experts feel that such randomized trials are the only good way to ascertain the efficacy of medical treatments. (See Box 19.)

9.8 Survey Research

Randomization is a very good way of demonstrating causation. But it is a mistake, notwithstanding the opinion of many in the medical establishment, to suppose that it is the *only* way. Sometimes it is simply not possible, for ethical or practical reasons, to conduct a randomized trial. Then we have to find out about causes the hard way. We need laboriously to survey the overall population and gather data on the correlation between putative cause and effect within subgroups of the population divided by gender, and income level, and stress,... and all the other things that could possibly be producing a spurious correlation. If none of these screens off the correlation, then this will give us reason to suppose that it reflects a causal connection.

Perhaps we can never be absolutely sure we have checked through every possible confounding factor. But sometimes we can be very confident. We will do well to remember the example of smoking and lung cancer. When the correlation between the two was first noticed, the cigarette companies were quick to suggest that it might be spurious, produced by some common cause like social class, or air pollution, or genetic factors, or ...

Now, there was no question of testing this by a randomized trial. (This would have been obviously unethical—you can't take a sample of children and force half of them chosen at random to be smokers.) But this doesn't mean we don't now know that smoking causes cancer. And the way we found out was precisely by surveying all the remotely plausible confounding factors, and showing that none of them in fact screens off the smoking–cancer correlation.

9.9 Simpson's Paradox

Screening off occurs when a common cause is responsible for a positive correlation between two properties even though there is no direct causal connection between them. The lack of a causal connection is exposed by the correlation *disappearing* when we control for the common cause.

There can also be cases where a common cause produces a positive correlation between two properties even though one is in reality a *negative* causal influence on the other. When we control for the common cause the correlation is *reversed*, and what at first looked like a positive cause turns out to have the opposite effect.

Take once more the positive correlation between heart disease (H) and alcohol consumption (A) which initially made it seem that drinking causes heart disease. We earlier supposed that when we controlled for gender and divided the population into females (F) and males (not-F), the correlation would disappear. But now imagine that controlling for gender actually reverses the correlation—that *within* each gender there is *less* heart disease among the drinkers than the rest.

$$Pr(H/A \text{ and } F) < Pr(H/F)$$

and

$$Pr(H/A \text{ and not-F}) < Pr(H/\text{not-F}).$$

Box 19 The Logic of Randomized Trials

In a 'randomized clinical trial' of a medical treatment we take a sample of patients with some ailment and divide them into two groups at random. The 'treatment' group is given the treatment and the 'control' group is not. We then observe whether the recovery rate in the treatment group is significantly higher than in the control group.

The rationale for such trials is to eliminate the danger of spurious correlations. In the wider world, perhaps young people, who are likely to recover anyway, are receiving the treatment more often than old people, and this is creating the impression that the treatment aids recovery. By randomizing the treatment, we forcibly decorrelate it from any such confounding causes as patient age.

Of course, if a treatment does appear efficacious in a particular trial, this could still be due to *statistical fluctuations*. Perhaps by luck the treatment group contained more people who were going to recover anyway. However, this statistical danger is present in any attempt to infer underlying patterns from finite samples, whether or not randomization is involved. And the standard remedy for this statistical danger is to use bigger samples to diminish the probability of misleading fluctuations.

But note that bigger samples are no guard against systematically confounding causes. Suppose that age does indeed influence both recovery and who gets the treatment. Simply getting bigger samples from the population at large isn't going to make this confounding influence go away.

Randomization guards against hidden confounding causes. Big samples guard against statistical fluctuations. Both help to ensure that our inferences are secure.

This would indicate that drinking actually does something to *prevent* heart disease, and only seems initially to cause it because it is more prevalent among men who are prone to heart disease anyway.

This kind of correlation reversal is widely referred to as '*Simpson's paradox*'. But in fact there is nothing terribly paradoxical about such examples. They are quite analogous to ordinary screening off. In both cases, some property appears initially to be a positive cause only because it is itself positively associated with the real cause. The only difference is that in ordinary cases of screening off the putative cause has no real influence at all, whereas in examples of Simpson's 'paradox' it is actually a negative cause.

FURTHER READING

Judea Pearl's *Causality: Models, Reasoning and Inference* (Cambridge University Press 2000) is a detailed study of the relationship between causes and correlations.

There is a useful section on 'Causal Modelling' in Christopher Hitchcock's Stanford Encyclopedia entry on Probabilistic Causation: <http://plato.stanford.edu/entries/causation-probabilistic>.

There is also a Stanford Encyclopedia entry specifically on Simpson's Paradox by Gary Malinas and John Bigelow: <http://plato.stanford.edu/entries/paradox-simpson>.

John Worrall offers an informative critical discussion of the logic of randomized trials in 'Why There's No Cause to Randomize', *The British Journal for the Philosophy of Science* 2007.

EXERCISES

1. When a fair die is thrown, what is the conditional probability of:

   (a) an even number, given a number less than three
   (b) an odd number, given an number greater than three
   (c) a number greater than three, given an odd number
   (d) a number greater than two, given an even number
   (e) a number greater than or equal to two, given a multiple of three
   (f) a multiple of three, given an even number?

2. For each of (a)–(f) in question 1, say whether the two results are independent, positively dependent, or negatively dependent.

3. Which is the odd one out?

   (a) $Pr(p/q) > Pr(p)$
   (b) $Pr(p\&q) > Pr(p)Pr(q)$
   (c) $Pr(\text{not-}p/q) > Pr(\text{not-}p)$
   (d) $Pr(\text{not-}p \& \text{not-}q) > Pr(\text{not-}p)Pr(\text{not-}q)$

4. Specify that p and q are probabilistically positively dependent in six different ways.

5. Suppose that the probability of having diabetes (D), being male (M), and being unemployed (U) are given by

Prob (D) = 0.05
Prob (M) = 0.60
Prob (U) = 0.30

And suppose that

Prob (D&M) = 0.024
Prob (U&D) = 0.018
Prob (U&M) = 0.18

For each of these last three pairs of properties, say whether the two properties are positively dependent, negatively dependent, or independent. For each of the pairs, work out the conditional probability of the first given the second.

6. Suppose that research shows that Pr(nose cancer/smoking) = 0.3 while Pr(nose cancer) = 0.1.

Research also shows that:

Pr(nose cancer/smoking & city-dwelling) = Pr(nose cancer/city-dwelling) = 0.4

and

Pr(nose cancer/smoking & country-dwelling) = Pr(nose cancer/country-dwelling) = 0.05.

What does all this indicate about the causes of nose cancer?

7. Suppose that research in the State University of Euphoria shows that Pr(successful entrance application/male) = 0.4 while Pr(successful entrance application/female) = 0.3.

Suppose also that the University deals separately with entrance applications to the Arts and Science Faculties, and that further research shows that:

Pr(successful entrance application/male & Arts) = 0.2 while Pr(successful entrance application/female & Arts) = 0.25

and

Pr(successful entrance application/male & Science) = 0.5 while Pr(successful entrance application/female & Science) = 0.6

What does all this indicate about the factors influencing application success?

Part IV
LOGICS AND THEORIES

10

. . . . .

Syntax and Semantics

10.1 Validity

Logic is to do with *arguments*.

An argument starts with some statements—the *premises*—and then takes us via a series of steps to another statement—the *conclusion*.

Arguments are designed to expand our knowledge. If you already know the premises, then a good argument will lead you to knowledge of the conclusion too.

Given this function, what we want of an argument is that the truth of its premises should *guarantee* the truth of its conclusion. An argument satisfying this desideratum is called *valid*.

Note that the validity of an argument doesn't require that the premises and conclusion actually be true—only that the conclusion must be true *if* the premises are true.

For example, consider this argument:

All Australians like cricket
Mel Gibson is Australian

_____

Mel Gibson likes cricket

Now, you might wonder whether the premises and conclusion of this argument are in fact true. But you don't need to settle this to know that the argument is valid. You can see that the premises guarantee the conclusion all right—in that the conclusion would be true *if* the premises were—independently of whether these statements actually are true.

It is not the job of an argument, so to speak, to check that its premises are true. That comes from outside the argument. The argument is solely concerned with the move *from* the premises *to* the conclusion, and it will have played its part as long as the truth of the former guarantees the truth of the latter.

10.2 Logic and Metalogic

We can regard logic as a skill, something we can be better or worse at. In this sense good logicians are people who are sensitive to the difference between valid arguments and invalid ones, and who go in for valid argumentation themselves. Some elementary logic courses are designed to improve this kind of skill. They aim to turn their students into valid arguers.

So construed, logic has no special subject matter. It is a generic skill that can be used—and should be used—in any area of thought. It is good for engineers and lawyers to be good logicians in this sense, as well as philosophers.

But we can also regard logic as an object of study. We can think *about* different ways of arguing validly, and analyse their workings. When we do this we are doing *metalogic*.

Metalogic, unlike logic, has a quite specific subject matter—the workings of logical arguments. Metalogic is of great interest to philosophers and mathematicians, but not necessarily to lawyers and chemists.

When philosophers and mathematicians talk about a 'good logician', they are likely to mean someone who knows a lot of metalogic—knows a lot *about* logical arguments—and not just someone who is good at arguing logically.

This chapter and the next two will contain some metalogic. This won't be designed to improve your argumentative skills. Rather my aim will be to introduce you to some philosophically interesting facts about logical arguments.

10.3 Different Kinds of Logic

We can classify logical arguments according to the way their validity depends on the meaning of certain logical constructions.

In studying *propositional* logic, we are concerned with arguments whose validity depends on the meanings of the '*truth-functional connectives*'—'not', 'and', 'or', and so on.

In studying *predicate* logic, we are further concerned with arguments whose validity depends on the meanings of the '*quantifiers*'—'for all x,...' and 'there is an x such that,...'.

Other branches of logic, such as 'second-order logic' and 'modal logic', involve arguments whose validity depends on the meaning of yet further constructions.

10.4 Truth-Functional Connectives

Let us stick to propositional logic for the moment. We shall consider some of the other branches of logic in the next chapter.

The 'truth-functional connectives' of propositional logic are specifically those words that can be used to make new sentences out of old ones in such a way that the truth or falsity of the new sentences is entirely determined by the truth and falsity of the old ones.

So given any sentence p, 'not'-p can be defined as a new sentence which is true if and only if p is false.

Similarly, given any two sentences p, q, p-'and'-q can be defined as a new sentence which is true if and only if p is true and q is true.

Again, p-'or'-q (with 'or' understood as 'and/or') can be defined as a new sentence which is true if and only if at least one of p and q is true.

And I will say that p-'→'-q can be defined as a new sentence which is true if and only if either p is false or q is true. (This is the material conditional discussed at the end of chapter 8. I'll come back to this one in a second.)

I have given these definitions in words, but they can be made graphic by the 'truth tables' that will be familiar to anyone who has done an elementary logic course. These truth tables illustrate directly how the truth values of the relevant complex sentences depend on the truth values of their constituents. (See Box 20.)

'Not', 'and', 'or', and '→' aren't the only truth-functional connectives, but they are enough for our purposes.

I have just offered 'definitions' of the words 'not', 'and', and so on. But of course it's not up to me to choose their meanings. They are already words of English with a life of their own, so to speak. So it is a substantial question whether the definitions I have offered are faithful to the meanings they already have.

And indeed there are respects in which the relevant English words do have connotations which go beyond the above definitions. Still, it will not hurt to ignore that here in the interests of simplicity.

The one exception is with the connective I have written as p-'→'-q. It is normal in introductions to logic to equate this with the English construction 'if p, then q'. But, as I explained in chapter 8, there is a quite substantial divergence between the logicians' p-'→'-q and the ordinary language 'if p, then q'. In recognition of this, I shall stick to the artificial '→' in this chapter.

Box 20 Truth Tables

....

The truth tables for 'not', 'and', 'or', and '→' show graphically how the truth values of the complex sentences we can make using these words depend on the truth values of their constituent sentences.

p	'not'-p
T	F
F	T

p	q	p-'and'-q
T	T	T
T	F	F
F	T	F
F	F	F

p	q	p-'or'-q
T	T	T
T	F	T
F	T	T
F	F	F

p	q	p-'→'-q
T	T	T
T	F	F
F	T	T
F	F	T

10.5 Syntax and Semantics

A central aim of metalogic is to construct a precise analysis of *logical consequence*—the relationship that some sentences (the premises) have to another (the conclusion) when the latter follows validly from the former.

One thing that makes metalogic interesting is that there are two different ways of thinking about logical consequence—*syntactically* and *semantically*.

When we analyse logical consequence *syntactically*, we think of argumentation as governed by a system of rules for moving between sentences of certain forms. One sentence is the logical consequence of some others if the rules allow you to construct a 'proof' in the sense of a sequence of legitimate moves that take you from the premises to the conclusion. From this syntactic perspective, the meanings of the sentences do not matter. Argumentation is viewed as nothing more than a *game* governed by certain *rules* for manipulating strings of symbols.

The *semantic* perspective, by contrast, attends to meanings rather than moves. Now we think of sentences not just as strings of symbols, but as meaningful statements which make claims that are true or false. And this allows us to view one sentence as a logical consequence of others if and only if their meanings are so related that the former sentence must be true if the latter are. From the semantic perspective, logical consequence is nothing to do with argumentative *moves*. It's simply a matter of all circumstances in which the premises are true being ones in which the conclusion is true too.

In the next two sections I shall illustrate these two different ways of understanding logical consequence in the case of propositional logic.

10.6 Syntactic Consequence

So let us first view propositional logic syntactically, as a game with certain rules. The most natural way to specify the rules is to list a set of *rules of inference*. Each rule of inference will allow you to move from sentences of certain forms to another sentence of a related form.

For example, here are two nice simple rules:

Given any two sentences p, q, you can move to p-'and'-q
Given any sentence of the form p-'and'-q, you can move to p (and similarly to q)

We can give a similar pair of rules for each of our other truth-functional connectives, the first of which allow us to move *from* sentences without the connective *to* sentences containing it (an '*introduction*' rule) and the other which allows us to move *from* sentences containing the connective *to* sentences without it (an '*elimination*' rule). (See Box 21.)

Once we have specified a set of rules of inference, we can then define a *proof*. A proof is a way of moving by steps from a set of premises to a conclusion using the rules of inference. More formally, a *proof* consists of an initial set of sentences given as *premises*, followed by a sequence of sentences each of which can be reached by the rules of inference from the premises plus other sentences earlier in the sequence. The last sentence in such a sequence is the *conclusion*. (See Box 22.)

This now gives us enough to define a syntactic notion of logical consequence for propositional logic. A sentence j is a syntactic consequence of a set of sentences K in propositional logic if there is a proof with premises K and conclusion j.

In such a case we write K $\vdash_{PROP}$ j, and we say that j is *provable* from K in propositional logic.

If we can prove j from zero premises, we write $\vdash_{PROP}$ j and say that j is *provable* simpliciter, or that j is a *theorem* of propositional logic.

(If you are puzzled about how anything can be proved from zero premises, have a look at the rule of Conditional Proof in the Box 21 below.)

Box 21 Inference Rules for Propositional Logic

....

'And' Introduction
Given p, q, move to p-'and'-q

'And' Elimination
Given p-'and'-q, move to p (or to q)

'Or' Introduction
Given p (or given q), move to p-'or'-q

'Or' Elimination
Given p-'or'-q, p-'→'-r , q-'→'-r, move to 'r'

Reductio Ad Absurdum ('Not' Introduction)
Given p-'→'-q, p-'→'-not-q, move to 'not'-p

Double 'Not' Elimination
Given 'not'-'not'-p, move to p.

Modus Ponens ('→' Elimination)
Given p, p-'→'-q, move to q.

Conditional Proof ('→' Introduction)
If assuming p allows you to move via this set of Inferential Rules to q, then you can move to p-'→'-q without assuming p.

10.7 Semantic Consequence

Note how nothing in the syntactic approach to propositional logic just outlined appeals to the meanings of sentences. From the syntactic perspective, the sentences may just as well be meaningless marks, and the inference rules may as well just specify the allowed moves in some arbitrary game.

But of course sentences aren't just meaningless marks—they express propositions which are true or false. To take this into account is to view the sentences *semantically*.

I have already explained, in section 10.4 above, how the truth-functional connectives can be viewed as devices which function to generate complex sentences whose *truth values* (their truth or falsity) are *determined* by the *truth values* of their constituents. This gives us a *semantic* understanding of sentences involving truth-functional connectives. We see how the truth values of these sentences depend on the truth values of their simpler parts.

Box 22 An Example of a Syntactic Proof

....

Here is a proof of 'not'-p from p-'→'-q and 'not'-q.

  (1) Premise   p-'→'-q
  (2) Premise   'not'-q

Suppose we now *assume* p

We were given 'not'-q as a premise

So *assuming* that *p* allows us to move to 'not'-q.

So without assuming *p* we can move, via '→' *Introduction*, to

  (3)   p-'→'-'not' -q

And from (1) and (3) we can move to

  (4)   'not'-p   by 'Not' Introduction.

Once we are armed with this semantic grasp of the truth-functional connectives, we can approach the issue of logical consequence from a semantic rather than a syntactic perspective. Instead of asking whether we can *move* from some sentences to another via the specified rules of inferences, we can simply ask whether their meanings are so related that the latter *must be true* if the former *are true*.

So, for example, suppose we are interested in whether some sentence 'not'-p is a logical consequence of p-'→'-q and 'not'-q. Then we can easily see, by attending to the relevant truth tables, that the conclusion must indeed be true if the premises are. (See Box 23.)

This illustrates the semantic notion of logical consequence for propositional logic. A sentence j is a semantic consequence of a set of sentences K in propositional logic if and only if the definitions of the truth-functional connectives ensure that j must be true whenever the sentences in K are all true.

In such cases we write $K \vDash_{PROP} j$, and we say that j is a *semantic* consequence of K in propositional logic.

If j must be true whatever is the case, then we write $\vDash_{PROP} j$, and we say that j is a propositional *logical truth*.

For example any sentence of the form p-'or'-'not'-p is a propositional logical truth. The semantic definitions of 'or' and 'not' ensure that any such sentence is true whatever p says.

Now that we have explained and contrasted the syntactic and semantic notions of logical consequence, we can ask about their relationship to each other. That will be the subject of the next chapter.

Box 23 An Example of Semantic Consequence

....

The following truth table shows that 'not'-p is a semantic consequence of
p-'→'-q and 'not'-q: the bottom row represents the only case where p-'→'-q
and 'not'-q are both true—and in that row 'not'-p is also true

p	q	p-'→'-q	'not'-q	'not'-p
T	T	T	F	F
T	F	F	T	F
F	T	T	F	T
F	F	T	T	T

FURTHER READING

There are many excellent elementary logic textbooks, including Wilfried Hodges' *Logic* (Penguin 2nd edition 2001) and Paul Tomassi's *Logic* (Routledge 1999).

The elementary book that pays most attention to metalogical issues is still the classic *Beginning Logic* by E.J. Lemmon (Nelson 1965).

The Logic Manual by Volker Halbach (Oxford University Press 2010) also has a usefully metalogical slant.

EXERCISES

1. Give examples of valid arguments with:

    (a) true premises and true conclusion
    (b) false premises and false conclusion
    (c) false premises and true conclusion

    Why haven't I asked for an example with true premises and false conclusion?

2. Use truth tables to show that the following are logically true: p-'or'-'not'-p; 'not'-(p-'and'-'not'-p); (p-'and'-'not'-p-)'→'-q.

3. Which of the following claims are true? (Indicate your reasons for your answer.)

    (a) 'not'-(p-'and'-'not'-q), 'not'-p $\models$ q
    (b) $\models$ ((p-'or'-'not'-q)-'and'-q)-'→'-p
    (c) $\vdash$ p-'→'-(p-'or'-q)
    (d) $\vdash$ p-'→'-(p-'and'-q)

4. State three rules of inference from propositional logic and use the truth tables for the connectives involved to show that their conclusions must be true if their premises are.

5. Use the definitions of K $\models_{PROP}$ q and $\models_{PROP}$ q and the truth table for '→' to explain why: p $\models_{PROP}$ q if and only if $\models_{PROP}$ p → q.

11

· · • · ·

Soundness and Completeness

11.1 Soundness and Completeness

At the end of the last chapter I outlined two quite different ways of characterizing logical consequence in propositional logic. The syntactic characterization paid no attention to the meanings of sentences—it was only concerned with whether you can move from some sentences to others via the rules of inference. Conversely, the semantic characterization paid no attention to the rules of inference—it was only concerned with whether the meanings of sentences are related in such a way that the truth of some guarantees the truth of others.

Given this, we can ask how the two characterizations are related.

In particular, we can ask whether every case of syntactic consequence is also a case of semantic consequence. That is, can we construct proofs *only* in cases where the truth of the premises in fact guarantees the truth of the conclusion? If this is so, we say that the syntactic rules of inference are *sound*.

Conversely, we can ask whether every case of semantic consequence is also a case of syntactic consequence. That is, can we construct a proof in *every* case where the truth of the premises guarantees the truth of the conclusion? If this is so, we say that the syntactic rules of inference are *complete*.

In asking whether the rules of inference are sound, we are asking whether they are good ways of moving from premises to conclusions. Rules of inference that were *not* sound would allow us to construct 'proofs' whose conclusions were not guaranteed by their premises.

In asking whether the rules of inference are complete, we are asking whether they cover *all* the good ways of moving from premises to conclusions. Do they license a proof in *every* case where the truth of some sentences guarantees the truth of another? Rules of inference that were *not* complete would *not* allow us to construct proofs of some sentences whose truth *was* guaranteed by that of other sentences.

11.2 Proving Soundness and Completeness

As it happens, the rules of inference given above for propositional logic are both sound and complete.

It is easy enough to show that these rules of inference are *sound*.

To establish soundness, we first go through the rules of inference in turn and appeal to the semantic definitions of the relevant connectives to show that none of them can take us from truths to falsehoods.

So, for example, consider our first rule of inference, 'And' Introduction, which says *given p, q, move to p-'and'-q*. Since the semantic definition of 'and' tells us that p-'and'-q is true if both p and q are true, we can see that this rule must take us to a true conclusion whenever its premises are true.

It is straightforward to show that all the propositional rules of inference must similarly have true conclusions if their premises are true.

Since a proof in propositional logic is a sequence of sentences generated from a set of premises by repeatedly applying these rules of inference, it now follows that any such propositional proof must itself have a true conclusion if its premises are true—given that no rule of inference can take us from truths to falsehoods, repeatedly applying the rules of inference must keep us on the track of truth if we start there. And this then establishes soundness—if one sentence is a syntactic consequence of some others (that is, it is provable from them), then it must be a semantic consequence too (that is, its truth must be guaranteed by their truth).

Establishing the *completeness* of the rules of inference is harder.

Now we need to show, not that provability implies semantic consequence, but that semantic consequence implies provability—that is, that *some* proof exists whenever the truth of one sentence is ensured by the truth of some others. There are various ways of showing this, but they are all a bit complicated. If you are interested in following this up, I refer you to the Further Reading at the end of the chapter.

11.3 Reflections on Circularity

When we consider whether the propositional rules of inference are sound and complete, we are in effect *evaluating* them. We are seeing how far they are well designed for valid argumentation. Do they indeed serve their basic function of leading us from truths to truths?

Thus, in asking whether the rules are sound, we are checking that they license proofs *only* when the truth of the premises in fact guarantees the truth of the conclusion. And in asking whether they are complete, we are checking whether they *always* license proofs in such cases.

It is a bit weird, if you think about it, that we can evaluate our rules of inference in this way.

After all, the rules of inference listed earlier were not some random set of procedures pulled out of a hat. While I invited you to view them as the rules in a meaningless game, they weren't in truth selected haphazardly. Rather they were designed to capture the way that sensible people argue. That is, they were a summary of the best practice of 'good logicians'—in the earlier sense of people with good argumentative skills.

But how then was it possible to 'evaluate' these rules by considering their soundness and completeness? After all, when we show that the rules are sound and complete, we are simply *arguing* that they have certain good qualities. That is, we are *using* normal rules of inference to conclude that those selfsame rules are good ones. (In the last section I didn't actually display detailed demonstrations of propositional soundness and completeness, but simply indicated how they might be given. However, if we did examine the details of such demonstrations, they would undoubtedly appeal to rules like Reductio ad Absurdum, Modus Ponens, and so on at various points.)

However, this would then seem to mean we are evaluating normal argumentative skills by appeal to those selfsame argumentative skills. How could this circular exercise be of any significance?

But look at it like this. When we adopt the syntactic perspective, and lay out the rules of inference, we are viewing logic from the inside, so to speak. We are describing the internal structure of our argumentative practice, by specifying the kinds of transitions between sentences that we engage in when we argue.

But when we adopt the semantic perspective we stand back and view this argumentative practice from the outside. Now sentences are not just positions in an argumentative game, but items which report on the real world, and so are either true or false. This external perspective then allows us to assess how far our argumentative practice is indeed well suited to moving us from truths to truths.

This exercise can be genuinely illuminating. We can see that our rules of inference are not just arbitrary conventions adopted by society, like holding your fork in your left hand. Rather there is a very good reason to use these rules of inference. Their premises and conclusions are semantically related in ways that ensure their conclusions are true if their premises are.

This is not to deny that there is some element of circularity involved in demonstrations of soundness or completeness. We are indeed *using* our argumentative skills—our rules of inference—in carrying out these demonstrations. And this means that there is no question of using them to *persuade* people who lack these skills that they ought to acquire them. Somebody who doesn't already engage in the relevant rules of inference won't be moved by a demonstration that they are good rules of inference.

But this doesn't mean that these demonstrations have no significance for those of us who do possess normal argumentative skills. On the contrary, they enable us to understand *why* it is good to reason in line with our rules of inference.

For instance, consider 'modus ponens', the rule that licenses moves from p and p-'→'-q to conclusion q. Note that you could *practice* this rule without ever having thought *about* it. In particular you might never have asked yourself why it is a good thing to go in for. Moreover, once you do ask this question, you may not immediately see how to answer it.

But attention to the semantic definition of '→' allows a genuinely informative answer. p-'→'-q is true as long as either p is false or q is true. So the only way p-'→'-q can be true when p is true is for q to be true too. So modus ponens, in taking us from p and p-'→'-q to q, can never take us from truths to a falsehood. *That's* why it is a good idea to conform to this rule.

11.4 Predicate Logic

Let us go back to an example from the beginning of the last chapter (now rewritten a bit more formally):

(For all x)(x is Australian → x likes cricket)

Mel Gibson is Australian
_____

Mel Gibson likes cricket

As I said, this is a valid argument. But its validity isn't just a matter of truth-functional connectives. It also depends on the way that the argument involves *universal quantification*—'(For all x)(...)'.

Here is another example.

John is tall

John is fat
_____

(There is an x such that)(x is tall and fat)

Here the validity of the argument depends on its use of *existential quantification*—'(There is an x such that)(...)'.

Predicate logic is concerned with arguments whose validity depends on universal and existential quantification, as well as on the truth-functional connectives. (We can think of predicate logic as *including* propositional logic but adding some further structure.)

Just as with propositional logic, we can analyse logical consequence in predicate logic both *syntactically* and *semantically*.

11.5 Predicate Syntax

To get a syntactic account of logical consequence for predicate logic, we need to add some extra rules of inference for the quantifiers to those for the truth-functional connectives. In particular, we need introduction and elimination rules for both the universal and existential quantifier.

These are a bit messy to state precisely, so let me just give the general idea.

To understand the elimination rule for universal quantification, note that what goes for everything goes for any particular thing. A rough version of the rule is thus:

Given a condition F and a name a, you can move from '(For all x)(x is F)' to 'a is F'.

To understand the introduction rule for existential quantification, note that what goes for a particular thing goes for something. A rough version of the rule is thus:

Given a condition F and a name a, you can move from 'a is F' to '(There is an x such that)(x is F)'.

The other two rules are a bit harder to grasp. The introduction rule for universal quantification says that:

If, given some condition F, you can prove 'a is F' whatever name a is used, then you can move to '(For all x)(x is F)'.

(The idea is that a condition must apply to everything if there is a proof which can show it applies to any particular thing.)

And the elimination rule for existential quantification says that:

You can move from '(There is an x such that)(x is F)' to a sentence p, if p can be proved from 'a is F' whatever name a is used.

(The idea is that if p follows from an arbitrary object's satisfying a condition F, then it must follow from *something* satisfying F.)

Once we have specified a set of rules of inference, we can define notions of proof and syntactic consequence for predicate logic just as we did for propositional logic. A sentence j is a syntactic consequence of a set of sentences K in predicate logic if there is a proof in predicate logic with premises K and conclusion j. In such a case we write K $\vdash_{PRED}$ j, and we say that j is *provable* from K in predicate logic. And if we can prove j from zero premises, we write $\vdash_{PRED}$ j and say that j is *provable* simpliciter, or that j is a *theorem* of predicate logic.

11.6 Predicate Semantics

Just as the syntax for predicate logic expands the syntax for propositional logic, so does its semantics expand propositional semantics. In the last chapter we saw how the truth values of sentences with truth-functional structure depend on the semantic values of their parts. Predicate semantics adds to this propositional semantics a further explanation of how the truth values of sentences with *quantificational* structure similarly depend on the semantic values of their parts.

To achieve this, we suppose that there is some set of objects at issue when we say '(For all x)(...)' or '(There is an x)(...)'. This set is called 'the domain of discourse'. We then further suppose that all names refer to some object in this domain, and that all predicates are associated with some subset of this domain.

We can then say that, given any name *a* and predicate *F*, a sentence of the form '*a* is *F*' will be true if and only if the object named by *a* is a member of the set associated with *F*.

And we can also say that any sentence of the form '(For all x)(x is *F*)' will be true if and only if everything in the domain of discourse is in the set associated with *F*.

Similarly, any sentence of the form '(There is an x)(x is *F*)' will be true if and only if something in the domain of discourse is in the set associated with *F*.

(I am here skating over some technicalities that arise from the fact that quantified sentences can involve *complex* conditions constructed by applying truth-functional connectives to *predicates*, whereas so far we have only dealt with the semantic contribution of truth-functional connectives to complex *sentences*. But the above is already enough to give the general idea of predicate semantics.)

Again, once we are armed with a semantics for predicate logic, we can define a notion of semantic consequence for predicate logic just as we did for propositional logic. A sentence j is a semantic consequence of a set of sentences K in predicate logic if and only if the semantics for predicate logic ensures that j must be true whenever the sentences in K are all true. In such cases we write K $\vdash_{PRED}$ j, and we say that j is a *semantic* consequence of K in predicate logic. And if the semantics ensures that j will be true whatever is the case, then we write $\vdash_{PRED}$ j, and we say that j is a *logical truth* in predicate logic.

11.7 Predicate Logic—Soundness and Completeness

Just as with propositional logic, predicate logic can be shown to be both sound and complete. It can be proved that every case of syntactic consequence is also a case of semantic consequence—so predicate logic is sound—and that every case of semantic consequence is also a case of syntactic consequence—so predicate logic is complete.

The proof of soundness for predicate logic is straightforward, but the proof of completeness for predicate logic takes us beyond the bounds of elementary metalogic. It was first proved by Kurt Gödel in 1929.

11.8 Predicate Logic—Undecidability

Even though predicate logic shares the properties of soundness and completeness with propositional logic, there is a different respect in which it is rather less tractable than propositional logic. Where propositional logic is '*decidable*', predicate logic is not.

Focus on the semantic notion of a logical truth explained earlier—a sentence that is guaranteed to be true whatever is the case. For example, any sentence of the form 'p or not-p' is a logical truth in propositional logic. And any sentence of the form '(For all x)(not-(Fx and not-Fx))' is a logical truth in predicate logic.

Now, there is an effective procedure for deciding whether or not any given sentence is a logical truth of propositional logic. If you have done an elementary logic course, you will have learnt how to apply 'truth table' or 'semantic tableaux' tests for propositional logical truth. These procedures are essentially mechanical. You could use them to program a computer to tell whether or not any given sentence is a propositional logical truth.

However, there is no such effective procedure for predicate logical truth. There is no mechanical way of telling in a finite time whether or not any given sentence is a logical truth of predicate logic.

This might seem odd. After all, there is a mechanical way of making a list of all the predicate logical truths. (You could set a computer to start constructing proofs by applying the rules of inference of predicate logic in some systematic order. This would then generate an infinite list of all the proofs, from which we could derive an infinite list of all the theorems of predicate logic, that is, all the sentences that are provable from zero premises. And since predicate logic is sound and complete, all and only the logical truths are theorems.[1] So this would give us a mechanically generated infinite list of all the logical truths.)

But a mechanically generated infinite list of all the logical truths does not amount to a procedure for telling *whether or not* any given

---

[1] I earlier defined soundness and completeness in terms of relations between syntactic and logical *consequence*. But we can also say that a logic is *sound* if all its *theorems* are *logical truths*, and *complete* if all its *logical truths* are *theorems*. The proof of the equivalence of these two pairs of definitions is not difficult but too messy to give here.

sentence p is a logical truth. You could of course start running through the list to see if p is there, but this procedure is not guaranteed to produce a result. True, if p *is* a logical truth, then you are sure to find this out by going down the list—after some finite time you are guaranteed to come to it. But if p is *not* a logical truth then going down the list won't tell you anything—for you will never be in a position to tell whether p is yet further down the list or just not there at all.

It would be different if we had an infinite list of both the logical truths *and* of the sentences which are *not* logical truths. For then we could run down both lists and be sure to find any given sentence on one of them after some finite time. However, there is no way to generate a list of all the *non*-logical-truths of predicate logic, in the way we can generate a list of the logical truths.

In cases like this, logicians say that the set of predicate logical truths is '*recursively enumerable*' but not '*recursive*'. The set is *recursively enumerable* because there is a mechanical procedure for producing a list of its members. But it is not *recursive* because there is no mechanical procedure for deciding whether or not any given item is a member. ('Recursive' in this context can be understood as equivalent to 'programmable'.)

The points made above imply that, for any set S, if both S *and* the set of things that are not in S are recursively enumerable, then S will be recursive.

11.9 Second-Order Logic

So far we have seen that both propositional logic and predicate logic are sound and complete. This might make you think that any logical system will be similarly sound and complete. However, this would be wrong. *Second-order* logic is not complete.

Second-order logic is concerned with arguments that involve 'quantification over properties'.

Consider this argument.

Bill has every property that Anne has
Anne is wise

Bill is wise

Or, a bit more formally

(For all ∅)(Anne is ∅ → Bill is ∅)
Anne is wise

Bill is wise

Again, consider this argument

Anne is tall
Bill is tall

There is a property that both Anne and Bill have

which can in turn be symbolized as

Anne is tall
Bill is tall

(There is a ∅ such that)(Anne is ∅ and Bill is ∅)

These look like valid arguments all right. But note that they are not captured by predicate logic. Predicate logic is concerned with 'first-order' existential and universal quantification over *objects*—items named in the subject position of simple sentences, like *Anne* in 'Anne is tall'. But predicate logic does not deal with 'second-order' quantification over *properties*.

So while predicate logic licenses the inference from

Anne is tall

to

(There is an × such that)(× is tall)

it does not recognize the inference from

Anne is tall

to

(There is a Ø such that)(Anne is Ø).

This last inference involves second-order *existential* quantification—that is, claims of the form '(There is a Ø such that)(…)'. We also saw above an example of second-order *universal* quantification—that is, a claim of the form '(For all Ø)(…)'.

11.10 The Incompleteness of Second-Order Logic

If we want to formalize second-order logic, we will need to add a syntax and semantics for the second-order quantifiers to the syntax and semantics already given for predicate logic. That is, we will need to specify a set of rules of inference for the second-order quantifiers. And we will need to explain how the truth values of sentences involving second-order quantifiers are determined by the semantic values of their parts.

Now, it is indeed possible to do this, roughly analogously to the way I explained how it is done for first-order existential and universal quantification above. (For example, you want a syntactic rule of inference that allows you to go from '*a* is *F* to '(There is a Ø such that)(*a* is Ø)'. And semantically we can specify that sentences of this latter form are true if and only if there is some subset of the domain of discourse to which *a* belongs. And so on.)

However, when we do specify a syntax and semantics along these lines, we don't end up with a set of rules of inference that is both sound and complete for second-order logic. Given the natural way of specifying a semantics for second-order quantification, *no* set of rules of inference can be both sound and complete. If we stick to rules that are sound—that is, will only take us from truths to truths—then they will inevitably fail to capture all cases of semantic consequence—there will be some sentences whose truth is guaranteed by other sentences but which cannot be reached from those others via the rules of inference.

The trouble is that the sentences whose truth is guaranteed by second-order semantics will always outrun those that are syntactically provable.

We saw in section 11.8, on the undecidability of predicate logic, that we can recursively enumerate the theorems of predicate logic, in the sense of sentences provable from zero premises. (We just program a computer to start applying the rules of inference in some systematic order.) In fact this works for any specified set of rules of inference. Since a computer could be programmed to apply any set of rules of inference in a systematic order, the theorems that they generate will be recursively enumerable.

However, the logical truths guaranteed by the standard semantics for second-order logic are *not* recursively enumerable. This means that there must be some that are not theorems.

FURTHER READING

Lemmon's *Beginning Logic* (Nelson 1965) contains proofs of soundness and completeness for propositional logic.

Geoffrey Hunter's *Metalogic* (University of California Press new edition 1992) is an excellent introduction by a philosopher to the meta-theory of first-order logic.

Computability and Logic by George Boolos and Richard Jeffrey (Cambridge University Press 1974) covers a great deal of metalogical ground from the perspective of computability theory.

Michael Dummett's 'The Justification of Deduction' (reprinted in his *The Logical Basis of Metaphysics*, Harvard University Press 1989) is the classic discussion of the circularity issues raised in section 11.3.

EXERCISES

There are no Exercises for this chapter.

12

. . . . .

Theories and Gödel's Theorem

12.1 Theories

In the last two chapters I discussed logic. Logic is to do with question of validity, to do with some sentences *following* from others. It tells us that we can believe certain sentences *if* we believe others. But it is not logic's job to tell us which sentences to believe in the first place.

Theories contrast with logic in this respect. Where logic aims at validity, theories aim at *truth*. A good theory is one whose sentences are true. So a good theory tells us that certain sentences are to be believed.

Different theories concern different aspects of the world. So, for example, Newton's theory concerns the way that forces influence the motion of physical objects, genetic theory concerns the mechanisms of heredity in organisms, Euclidean geometry concerns the size and shape of regions of space, Peano's theory concerns the natural numbers, and so on.

A theory will employ a *vocabulary* of non-logical terms to refer to its subject matter. So, for example, the vocabulary of Euclidean geometry will include 'point', 'line', 'distance', and 'angle'.

One way to formulate a theory is to specify a set of sentences as *axioms*. The theory then consists of all the sentences that follow by logic from those axioms. We call these sentences the *theorems* of the theory.

I shall assume henceforth that the logic in question here is first-order predicate logic.

(When I say 'follow by that logic', do I mean syntactic or semantic consequence? $\vdash_{PRED}$ or $\vDash_{PRED}$? Given that our logic is predicate logic, it doesn't matter. Predicate logic is both sound and complete, so we will get exactly the same set of theorems either way.)

Not all theories are actually formalized in this precise axiomatic way. You would be hard put to find an axiomatic version of contemporary genetic theory, say. But a number of theories of interest to mathematicians and logicians have well-known axiomatizations, including Euclid's axiomatization of geometry given in Chapter 4 and Peano's postulates for arithmetic. (See Box 24.)

12.2 Syntax and Semantics for Theories

Just as with logics, we can view axiomatic theories both syntactically and semantically.

When we view theories syntactically, we regard the theorems as nothing more than strings of meaningless marks arranged in specific ways.

But when we view theories semantically we interpret the sentences as having definite meanings. Not only do we assign meanings to the logical terms like 'not', 'or', and '(for all x)(....)', as in the last chapter. We also interpret the non-logical vocabulary as referring to definite entities in the real world. (So, for example, such non-logical vocabulary would include 'force' and 'mass' in Newtonian theory, 'gene' and 'chromosone' in genetic theory, 'line' and 'angle' in Euclidean geometry, and 'zero' and 'successor' in Peano's arithmetic.)

In the last chapter, adding semantics to syntax allowed us to ask whether logical systems were *sound* and whether they were *complete*.

With theories we can ask a similar pair of questions. We can ask whether theories are *sound* and whether they are *complete*.

But watch out—soundness and completeness for theories is different from soundness and completeness for logical systems. With logics these notions were focussed on the relation between syntax and *semantic consequence*. With theories they are focussed on the relation between syntax and *truth*.

Thus, in asking whether a theory is sound, we ask whether it includes as theorems *only* sentences which are *true*. A theory would fail on this score if it included as theorems some sentences that were false.

And in asking whether a theory is complete, we ask whether it includes as theorems *all* the *true* sentences that can be stated in its vocabulary. A theory would fail on this score if its theorems omitted some truths about its subject matter.

While these notions are now focussed on truth rather than logical consequence, note the analogy with the earlier definition for logics. With both theories and logics soundness requires that the syntax of the system do *only* what it should. And again in both cases completeness requires that the syntax of the system do *everything* that it should.

12.3 Theoretical Completeness

As I have just explained, completeness for theories is a semantic matter. Does the theory cover *all* the relevant truths? But somewhat curiously this semantic completeness has a purely 'internal' manifestation which we can specify without bringing in truth. If a

> **Box 24** Peano's Postulates
> ....
>
> The following five postulates about the natural numbers were proposed as
> the basis of arithmetic at the end of the nineteenth century by the Italian
> mathematician Giuseppe Peano (1858–1932).
>
> Postulate 1. 0 is a natural number
> Postulate 2. To each natural number n there corresponds a second natural number, called the
> successor of n.
> Postulate 3. For all n, 0 is not the successor of n.
> Postulate 4. If the successor of n = the successor of m, then n = m.
> Postulate 5. If a set S of natural numbers contains 0 and the successor of every number it contains,
> then it contains all the natural numbers.
>
> Together these postulates determine the structure of the natural numbers:
> 0 is the least natural number, distinct natural numbers have distinct succes-
> sors, and all the natural numbers are generated by starting with 0 and suc-
> cessively taking successors, so to speak.

theory is semantically complete, then for any sentence p that can be
stated in its vocabulary, either p or 'not'-p will be a theorem.

To see why, note that for any sentence p, one of p and 'not'-p will
always be true. But if a theory is complete, then its theorems cover all
the relevant truths. So one of p and 'not'-p must be a theorem.

Sometimes the property of having either p or 'not'-p as a theorem
for any p is called '*syntactic* completeness'. This is in recognition of the
fact that this property can be specified entirely in terms of the kind of
sentences that the theory contains and does not require us to mention
truth. By contrast, the property of having all truths as theorems is
called *semantic* completeness.

I have just explained that syntactic completeness is necessary for semantic completeness. If a theory includes all the truths, then it must have p or 'not'-p as a theorem for any relevant p. But of course syntactic completeness is not *sufficient* for semantic completeness. A theory could be radically wrong and yet take a definite view on every question that can be raised in its vocabulary. (In the extreme case, imagine a theory that included p as a theorem for every p that was *false*, and 'not'-p as a theorem for every p that was true.)

12.4 Completeness for Theories versus Completeness for Logics

I originally defined completeness for a logic as the requirement that every semantic consequence is a syntactic consequence (that is, if $K \models j$ then $K \vdash j$). But as I later observed (Chapter 11, footnote 1) it can alternatively be defined as the requirement that every logical truth is a theorem in the sense of being provable from zero premises (if $\models j$ then $\vdash j$).

The latter formulation better enables us to appreciate some important differences between completeness for theories and completeness for logics. In both cases, completeness is loosely speaking a matter of all the sentences with the right semantic property being theorems. But in the case of theories, this comes out as all the *true* sentences being theorems, while in the case of logics, this comes out as all the *logically true* sentences being theorems (that is, provable from nothing).

This is why there is nothing in the case of logics analogous to the internal syntactic completeness which manifests semantic completeness in the case of theories. We can't say that if a logic is complete, then either p or 'not'-p must be a theorem (in the way that if a theory is complete, then p or 'not'-p must be a theorem). And this is because a complete logic succeeds in capturing *logical* truth, not truth per se, and there is no requirement that either p or 'not'-p must always be logically true, in the way that either p or 'not'-p must always be true.

Plenty of sentences are such that neither they nor their negations are logically true. Take the sentence 'David Papineau has been to Moscow'. Either this sentence or 'David Papineau has not been to Moscow' must be true, because one must represent the world correctly. But neither has to be *logically* true. Logical truth is not just being true, but being *guaranteed* to be true. And while one of 'David Papineau has been to Moscow' and 'David Papineau has not been to Moscow' must indeed be true, neither one of them is *guaranteed* to be true.

12.5 Gödel's Theorem Stated

Gödel's theorem (more precisely, 'Gödel's first incompleteness theorem') shows that *no* sound theory for arithmetic can be complete.

For example, take the theory that has Peano's postulates as axioms. Assume it is sound—that is, that it contains no falsehoods. Gödel showed that there is then a true sentence that can be stated in the language of arithmetic, but which cannot be proved from Peano's postulates (or from any other reasonable attempt to axiomatize arithmetic).

This is a very striking result. It tells us that no sound axiomatic theory can capture all the truths of arithmetic. However many truths are captured by the axioms, there will always be some that escape.

In fact Gödel himself didn't just prove that no *sound* theory for arithmetic can be complete, but the interestingly stronger result that no *consistent* theory for arithmetic can be complete.[1] (His result is stronger

---

[1] More precisely, he originally proved that no arithmetical theory with a property called 'ω-consistency' can be complete, which isn't quite as strong as proving that no consistent arithmetical theory can be complete.

because soundness implies consistency, but consistency does not require soundness.) However, the proof sketched below for the weaker thesis avoids some tiresome technicalities, while still conveying the essential features of Gödel's original construction.

12.6 A Sketch of Gödel's Proof

To prove the theorem, we start by 'Gödel numbering' all the sentences that can be formulated within the vocabulary of Peano's theory of arithmetic. (See Box 25.) Gödel showed how to construct a system that will associate a unique natural number with any such sentence. The Gödel numbers thus serve as labels for the theory's sentences. (Different systems of Gödel numbering can be constructed, using different numbers as labels for the sentences. Let us assume that we have fixed on one such system.)

Gödel also showed how to associate a unique number with every *sequence* of sentences. (We will be interested in sequences of sentences because some such sequences will constitute *proofs* of their last members from Peano's axioms using predicate logic rules of inference.)

Given our system of Gödel-numbering, this *syntactic* relation of proof will be mirrored by a *numerical* relation between numbers—let us symbolize this as $m\,PRF\,n$—which holds if and only if m is the Gödel number of a sequence that proves the sentence whose Gödel number is n. Given this, we can think of the numerical relation PRF as *encoding* the syntactic relation of proof.

While PRF encodes the syntactic relation of proof, we should also hold in mind that PRF is an ordinary relation between numbers. For example, given some specific system of Gödel numbering, it might come out that the sequence numbered by m proves the sentence numbered by n if and only if $m^7 = n - 13$. (Of course, in any actual case it will be far more complicated than that. But the point remains that PRF will be some such ordinary numerical relation.)

Now, Gödel showed that this numerical relation *PRF* can itself be represented within the formal language of arithmetic. Within this language we can write down sentences 'm PRF n' which will be true if and only if the number *m* bears *PRF* to the number *n*. (This is where most of the hard work comes in his proof.)

Consider now any arithmetic sentence of this form:

K: '(There is no x such that)(x PRF k)'.

In effect, K *'says'* that the sentence with Gödel number *k* is unprovable. K will be true if and only if there is no sequence which proves the sentence with Gödel number *k*.

Of course, K doesn't strictly say that some sentence is unprovable. K is in the first instance an ordinary arithmetical claim. (Sticking with the illustration above, K comes out as '(There is no x such that)($x^7 = k - 13$)'). Still, we can happily view K as *encoding* the unprovability of the sentence with Gödel number *k*, given that K will be true if and only if this sentence is indeed unprovable.

Now we do something clever. Since sentences of the form K are at bottom just ordinary sentences of arithmetic, they themselves have Gödel numbers. Using this fact, Gödel showed that we can find some specific sentence of this form where *k* is the Gödel number of *that sentence itself*. We shall call this our 'Gödel sentence' and abbreviate it as G.

So G is the sentence

G: '(There is no x such that)(x PRF g)'

where *g* is the Gödel number of that same sentence.

Observe that G *'says'* of itself *I am not provable*. More precisely, observe that G is an arithmetical sentence that will be true if and only if there is no proof of that sentence itself.

The result now quickly follows. If G is true if and only if it has no proof, there are only two possibilities. G is true and it has no proof. Or G is *false* and it *does* have a proof. But the latter possibility is ruled out by our assumption of soundness—a sound theory contains no falsehoods. So the only option left is that G is a true sentence that is not provable in our theory. Quod erat demonstrandum.

To drive the point home, remember that the Gödel sentence isn't some esoteric philosophical claim. It's just a sentence of arithmetic. Thus, reverting to our earlier illustration, it could be the sentence '(There is no x such that)$(x^7 = 17,546 - 13)$' where 17,546 is the Gödel number of that very sentence.

And what we have done is figured out, by attending to our system of Gödel numbering, that this numerical sentence is true if and only if it has no proof. Which means that, if arithmetic is sound, then this straightforward arithmetic sentence must be unprovable and true— for the only alternative is for it to be provable and false, which would violate the soundness or arithmetic.

12.7 The Inescapability of Gödel's Theorem

Let us recapitulate. We started with a formal theory—Peano's arithmetic—designed to capture all the truths of arithmetic. And we have shown that it doesn't. There is some ordinary arithmetic truth that does not follow from Peano's axioms.[2]

You might feel that this reflects badly on Peano's particular set of axioms, rather than on the idea of formalized arithmetic as such. Isn't the obvious moral that Peano's axioms are too weak, and that we need to beef them up by adding some more axioms? In particular, what

---

[2] All right—we only showed this on the assumption that arithmetic is sound. But I shall drop this qualification from now on. No one seriously doubts that Peano's arithmetic is sound. Just look at the axioms. The problem is that they don't generate enough truths, not that they generate some falsehoods.

Box 25 A System of Gödel Numbering

....

Suppose we have a list of all the basic words and symbols in our language of arithmetic and that there are less than one hundred of them. Then we could use the list to associate each word or symbol with a unique pair of digits. For instance, the list might pair the words and symbols on the left with the pairs of digits on the right:

'0'	07	'n'	03
'successor'	65	'for'	88
'not'	13	'all'	25
'the'	75	'of'	42
'is'	24	','	23

Then we could associate a unique number with every sentence of arithmetic by simply concatenating in order the pair of digits associated with words and symbols in the sentence.

So for example the sentence

'For all n, 0 is not the successor of n'

would get the number

8825032307241375654203.

It is clear that this system will give each sentence its own natural number. Given any natural number, we can read off from its decimal representation what string of symbols (if any) it determines.

To associate a unique number with any *sequence* of sentences, we need to take a bit of care. If we simply string together the decimal representations of the Gödel numbers of the sentences in the sequence, then different sequences of related sentences could possibly end up with the same number. However, if we put double zeros—00s—between the decimal representations of the Gödel numbers of the sentences in the sequence, then each sequence of sentences will be sure to have its own natural number.

about simply adding G itself as an axiom? That would fix the unprovability all right.

But adding extra axioms won't make the incompleteness go away. To see why, note that the proof sketched above didn't depend on the details of Peano's theory. Rather it appealed to a general recipe which will work for any formal theory of arithmetic: number its sentences, construct a Gödel sentence as above, and so on.

The only point where the content of Peano's theory really mattered was where Gödel showed that the relation *PRF* could be represented within that theory. So Gödel's proof will apply to *any* formal theory of arithmetic that is powerful enough to represent this relation. That is why adding axioms won't make the incompleteness go away. Systematically adding axioms to a theory won't make it less powerful in this respect. If Peano's theory is strong enough to represent *PRF*, then so is Peano's theory plus G.

Of course, if we add our original G above to Peano's axioms, we won't have a theory with *that* G as a Gödel sentence. That G will now trivially be provable. But Gödel's procedure guarantees that there will now be some further sentence G^{new} that is true but doesn't follow even from the augmented axioms. (If you are wondering *why* we now get a *new* G^{new} out of Gödel's procedure, note that, even if we keep the same system of Gödel numbering, the addition of our original G as an axiom will change the relation of *PRF*, and so lead to a different Gödel sentence.)

12.8 Meta-Theorizing

Here is an obvious puzzle about Gödel's theorem. On the one hand the theorem shows that a certain sentence is *not provable*. Yet at the same time the theorem shows that this sentence is true—that is, the theorem itself *proves* that sentence. Doesn't this take away with one hand what it gives with the other? However can you prove a sentence in the course of showing it is not provable?

To sort this out we need to distinguish carefully between our *object theory* and our *meta-theory*.

Any given version of Gödel's theorem will focus on some specific formal theory of arithmetic like Peano's theory. This is our object theory. The language of this theory (the *object language*) refers to numbers and their arithmetic relations but nothing else.

When we say the Gödel sentence is *not provable*, we mean it is not a theorem of this object theory. It cannot be logically derived from the axioms of the object theory.

Our *meta-theory* is the theory within which we prove Gödel's theorem itself. The language of this theory (the *meta-language*) talks about more than numbers. In particular, it also talks *about* the object theory, and specifically about the syntax and semantics of the sentences it contains. We now *mention* the terminology that the object theory merely *uses*. So now we can talk, not just about numbers, but also about the sentences of the object language—and crucially about whether those sentences are true or not. Our meta-theory thus enables us to stand outside the object theory, as it were, and assess its success in describing its subject matter.

When, in the course of Gödel's theorem, we establish that G is true and so *prove* it, we are proving it within this meta-theory.

This is why there is nothing contradictory about Gödel's theorem. It shows us that G is not provable within the *object theory*, and at the same time proves it within the *meta-theory*.

It is pretty amazing that a sentence that is unprovable within Peano's theory, say, can be proved simply by adding to Peano's theory the ability to talk about the truth of its own sentences. But while this may be amazing, it is not contradictory.

Observe now how the move to a meta-theory does not allow us to escape the limitations imposed by Gödel's theorem, any more than just adding G as an axiom did. Just as adding G as an axiom gave rise to a new unprovable Gödel sentence, so does the move to a meta-theory.

True, by moving to a meta-theory we can prove our original G. But that meta-theory could itself be laid out as a formal system, and Gödel's procedure could then be applied to *that* system, and it would then generate some new true G^{meta} that can't be proved within the meta-theory.

True, we would now be working within a meta-meta-theory, and this last application of Gödel's procedure would now also prove our new G^{meta} within this meta-meta-theory. But that meta-meta-theory too could be formalized and Gödelized to generate a yet further true $G^{meta-meta}$ that it can't prove. And so on.

It is an interesting question exactly what moral to draw from all this. Gödel's theorem certainly shows that

(For all sound theories T)(there is some true sentence s such that T doesn't prove s)

But it would be a mistake to infer from this that

(There is a true sentence s such that)(for all sound theories T)(T does not prove s).

Even if every girl loves her own sailor, this doesn't mean that there is some particular sailor beloved by all girls. Similarly, even if every theory has its own unprovable truth, this doesn't mean that there is some particular truth that isn't provable in any theory.

FURTHER READING

Gödel's Proof (New York University press revised edition 2001) by Ernst Nagel and James R. Newman, originally published in 1958, is a classic introduction but now somewhat dated.

Peter Smith's *An Introduction to Gödel's Theorems* (Cambridge University Press 2007) is a detailed study written by a philosopher.

Roger Penrose's *Shadows of the Mind* (Oxford University Press 1994) explains Gödel's theorem in detail and then attempts to infer that the human brain is not a computer.

Douglas Hofstadter's *Gödel, Escher, Bach: The Eternal Golden Braid* (Basic Books 1979) also contains much interesting material on Gödel's theorem.

EXERCISES

There are no Exercises for this chapter.

SOLUTIONS TO EXERCISES

Chapter 1

1. (a) {Abe, Bertha, Carl}; (b) {1, 2, 5, 7, 11, 13}; (c) {x: x is a child aged 7–15}; (d) {France, Germany, Italy}; (e) {France, Germany, Italy, India, China}; (f) {x: lives in Europe}; (g) {x: x lives in China or Europe}; (h) {x: x weighs more than 7 kilos}.

2. (a) {Bertha}; (b) {5, 11, 13}; (c) {x: x is a child aged 10–12}; (d) {Germany, Italy}; (e) Ø; (f) {x: lives in Germany}; (g) Ø; (h) {x: x weighs more than 10 kilos}.

3. (a) Ø, {Abe}, {Bertha}, {Abe, Bertha}; (b) Ø, {7}, {8}, {9}, {7, 8}, {7, 9}, {8, 9}, {7, 8, 9}.

4. (a) {Ø, {1}, {7}, {1, 7,}}; (b) {Ø, {London}, {Manchester}, {Birmingham}, {London, Manchester}, {London, Birmingham}, {Manchester, Birmingham}, {London, Manchester, Birmingham}}.

5. (a) members: 2, 3; (b) subsets: {7,8}, {2,3}, Ø; (c) neither members nor subsets: {1, 2, 3, {7, 8}}.

6. (a) members: 2, {7,8}, {2,3}, 3; (b) subsets: {2,3}, Ø, {1, 2, 3, {7,8}}; (c) neither members nor subsets: none.

7. Suppose (A) is true; but then, given what it says, it must be false; so, by reductio, *(A) is not true*. Suppose (A) is not true; but then, given what it says, it must be true; so, by reductio, *(A) is true*. The two italicized claims compose a contradiction.

Chapter 2

1. Example: Philosophy students know how to spell 'philosophy'. Example: John didn't like being called 'John'. In both examples the relevant word is used first and mentioned second.

2. 2; 1; 10; 10.

3. For example:

| 0 | +5 | -5 | +10 | -10 | ... |
| 0 | 1 | 2 | 3 | 4 | ... |

4. (a) and (c).

5*. Look what happens when we divide 9 by 7, say $7\overline{)9.0000\ldots}$

7 into 9 goes 1, remainder 2;

7 into 20 goes 2, remainder 6;

7 into 60 goes 8 remainder 4;

7 into 40 goes 5, remainder 5;

7 into 50 goes 7, remainder 1;

7 into 10 goes 1, remainder 3;

7 into 30 goes 4, remainder 2;

7 into 20 goes 2, remainder 6

—and now we have started recurring and so have the answer 1.285714285...

In general, when we do a long-division computation $q\overline{)p.0000\ldots}$, there will be at most q distinct 'remainders'. And so once we are past the decimal point the answers will start repeating after at most q steps.

6*. Consider for example 9.25126126126...Take the 'recurring part' $r = 0.00126126126\ldots$ Multiply by 10^3 to get 1.26126126... Subtracting r from this leaves 1.26. So $(10^3 - 1)r = 1.26$, and $r = 126/999 = 14/111$. Adding this to 9 25/100 gives 9 167/444. In general, multiply the 'recurring part' r of any recurring decimal by 10^k, where k is the number of digits in the recurring part, subtract the original recurring part to get a non-recurring answer for $(10^k - 1)r$, and proceed as above.

Chapter 3

1. (a) infinity_0; (b) infinity_0; (c) 2^{infinity_0}.

2. Given any numerical list of decimal representations of all the rational numbers, you can certainly use Cantor's trick to construct a decimal representation that is not in that list. But you can't assume that this represents a *rational* number. (Indeed, we know, since the rationals are denumerable, that it *can't* represent a rational number. An interesting further exercise is to understand directly why the construction can't yield a recurring decimal. See <http://www.mathpages.com/home/kmath371.htm>.)

3. If we construct our new decimal representation, not by adding '1' to the nth digit of the nth number in the list, so to speak, but say by putting '6' if the nth digit of the nth number is '7', and '7' otherwise—then we can be sure that our new decimal representation doesn't end in an infinite strings of nines or zeros, and so that it uniquely determines a real number not represented in the original list.

4. The complication is that some real numbers have two binary representations, just as they have two decimal representations: thus in binary notation $0.01111\ldots = 0.1000\ldots$ To make sure that each real number determines a *unique* subset of the natural numbers, we need to specify that in such cases we use just one of the two representations, say the one ending in all zeros.

5*. A geometrical demonstration. Imagine bending the line segment from 0 to 1 into a semicircle with centre P. Then the rays projecting from P though the semicircle will pair up the points on the semicircle with the points on any infinitely long straight line parallel to the base of the semicircle.

An algebraic demonstration. The function $(1/x) - 2$ pairs up the points between 0 and $1/2$ with the positive real numbers, and the function $2 - (1/(x - (1/2)))$ pairs the points between $1/2$ and 1 with the negative real numbers.

Chapter 4

1. Some examples of analytic statements: *all squares have four sides; all women are female; if John is taller than Jim, then Jim is shorter than John.*

Some examples of synthetic statements: *there are no wild tigers in Africa; the Pope has been to Wembley stadium; copper conducts electricity.*

2. I'd say that (a), (c), and (g) are analytic, (b), (d), and (e) are synthetic, and that it's indeterminate which (f) and (h) are.

3. Syntheticity is a matter of meaning—a synthetic statement is one whose truth isn't guaranteed by the meanings of its terms. A posteriority is to do with knowledge—an a posteriori statement can only be known as a result of relevant experiences.

4. If a statement is analytic then its truth is guaranteed by the meanings of its terms; so someone who understands those terms will be in a position to know it without any further experiences—which means it is not a posteriori.

5. Some examples of claims that have been thought to be synthetic a priori: *every event has a cause; nothing can be red and green all over ; if a is heavier than b, and b heavier than c, then a is heavier than c;*… plus the claims of Euclidean geometry.

6. The claim at issue isn't (a) a matter of definition. Nor, if babies are born with the belief, is it (b) acquired from experience. But natural selection's ability to instil false beliefs as well as true ones is arguably a good reason for denying this belief the status of knowledge.

Chapter 5

1. Necessary: (a), (c), (e), (f); contingent: (b), (d), (g), (h).

2. An a posteriori necessity: *Marilyn Monroe = Norma Jeane Baker.* An a priori necessity: *Triangles have three sides.* An a priori contingency: *Julius (as defined in section 5.3) invented the zip.* An a posteriori contingency: *David Papineau is a philosopher.*

3. (c) and (e) are posteriori necessities; (a) and (f) are a priori necessities; (d) and (g) are a priori contingencies; (b) and (h) are a posteriori contingencies.

4. (a) is correct, because p's truth in all possible worlds implies its truth in at least one.

(b) is incorrect, because p's truth in one possible world does not imply its truth in all.

(c) is incorrect, because p's truth in all possible worlds does not imply it is not true in any.

(d) is correct, because p's truth in the actual world implies its truth in at least one.

(e) is incorrect, because p's falsity in the actual world does not imply its truth in at least one.

(f) is incorrect, because p's falsity in at least one possible world does not imply it is false in all.

(g) is correct, because p's falsity in all possible worlds implies not-p is true in all possible worlds.

5. (a), (e), and (f) are ruled out by logic and definitions; (b), (c), and (d) are ruled out by the essential properties of things.

6. (e), and (g) are naturally possible; (c), (f), and (h) are absolutely but not naturally possible; (a), (b), and (d) are neither.

Chapter 6

1. [NB these are not the only way of phrasing these alternative readings.] (a) (For each boy x)(there exists a teacher y such that)(x hates y), and (There exists a teacher y such that)(for every boy x)(x hates y); (b) (There exists a teacher x such that)(for every boy y)(x hates y) and (For each boy y)(there exists a teacher x such that)(x hates y); (c) (Necessarily)(the first mammal on the moon)(was human) and (The first mammal on the moon)(necessarily) (was human); (d) (Necessarily)(the tallest person in Britain) (is shorter than no one in Britain) and (The tallest person in Britain)(is necessarily)(shorter than no one in Britain); (e) (It might not have been that)(the head of the King's College London philosophy department is)(head of the King's College London philosophy department) and (The head of the King's College London philosophy department)(might not have been)(head of the King's College London philosophy department); (f) (It is not possible that)(the inventor of the zip)(did not invent the zip) and (The inventor of the zip)(couldn't possibly not have)(not invented the zip).

2. (c) first false, second true; (d) first true, second false; (e) first false, second true; (f) first true, second false.

3. (a) de re; (b) de dicto; (c) de re; (d) de dicto; (e) de re; (f) de re.

4. (a) true; (b) false; (c) true; (d) false; (e) true; (f) true.

5. (a) necessary; (b) necessary; (c) contingent; (d) contingent; (e) necessary; (f) necessary; (g) necessary; (h) contingent [Holland could have been a higher-lying country].

6. (a) a posteriori; (b) a priori; (c) a posteriori; (d) a priori; (e) a posteriori; (f) a priori; (g) a posteriori; (h) a posteriori.

Chapter 7

1. (a) $1/4$; (b) $1/13$; (c) $5/13$; (d) $3/4$; (e) $5/52$; (f) $1/2$; (g) 0.

2. (a) $1/16$; (b) $1/16$; (c) $4/16$; (c) $4/16$.

3. (a) $1/12$; (b) $1/6$; (c) $1/36$; (d) $1/2$; (e) $1/6$; (f) $5/18$; (g) $5/9$.

4. (a) 0.2 ; (b) 0.9; (c) 0.5.

5. Beach's expected utility = $(1 \times 10) + (0.5 \times \text{-}10) + (0.2 \times 20) = 10 - 5 + 4 = 9$.
   Cricket's expected utility = $(1 \times 15) + (0.3 \times \text{-}10) + (0.05 \times 20) = 15 - 3 + 1 = 13$.

6*. Since

(p or q) is logically equivalent to ((p & not-q) or (q))

and the propositions within the bracket on the right-hand side are incompatible, Kolmogorov's third axiom implies

(A) Pr(p or q) = Pr(p & not-q) + Pr (q).

And since

p is logically equivalent to ((p & q) or (p & not-q))

and the propositions within the bracket on the right-hand side are again incompatible, the third axiom also implies

$Pr(p) = Pr(p \& q) + Pr(p \& not\text{-}q)$

and hence

(B) $Pr(p \& not\text{-}q) = Pr(p) - Pr(p \& q)$.

(A) and (B) together give

$Pr(p \text{ or } q) = Pr(p) + Pr(q) - Pr(p \& q)$.

Chapter 8

1. $Pr(wind/rain) = 4/5$; $Pr(rain/wind) = 2/3$.

2. (a) 4/13; (b) 4/13; (c) 1/4; (d) 3/4; (e) 5/9; (f) 4/9; (g) 0.

3. 0.4 (= $Pr_{old}(h/e) = Pr_{old}(h) \times Pr_{old}(e/h)/Pr_{old}(e)$).

4. 0.2 (If h is the hypothesis that the coin is biased 75% in favour of Heads, and e the evidence that it landed Heads twice, $Pr_{old}(h) = 0.1$, $Pr_{old}(e/h) = 9/16$, $Pr_{old}(e)$ = $Pr_{old}(e/h)Pr_{old}(h) + Pr_{old}(e/not\text{-}h)Pr_{old}(not\text{-}h) = (9/16 \times 0.1) + (1/4 \times 0.9) = 9/32$. So $Pr_{old}(h/e) = 0.1 \times 9/16 \div 9/32 = 0.2$.)

5. (a) indicative; (b) subjunctive; (c) subjunctive; (d) indicative; (e) indicative; (f) subjunctive; (g) subjunctive; (h) indicative.

6. (a) true; (b) false; (c) false; (d) true; (e) false; (f) true; (g) (probably) false; (h) true.

Chapter 9

1. (a) 1/2; (b) 1/3; (c) 1/3; (d) 2/3; (e) 1; (f) 1/3.

2. (a) independent; (b) negatively dependent; (c) negatively dependent; (d) independent; (e) positively dependent; (f) independent.

3. (c) is the odd one out, as it specifies that p and q are negatively dependent, where the other inequalities specify that they are positively dependent.

4. Here are sixteen different ways of specifying that p and q are positively dependent:

Pr(p/q) > Pr(p), Pr(p/q) > Pr(p/not-q), Pr(q/p) > Pr(q), Pr(q/p) > Pr(q/not-p), Pr(p & q) > Pr(p)Pr(q); Pr(not-p/not-q) > Pr(not-p), Pr(not-p/not-q) > Pr(not-p/q), Pr(not-q/not-p) > Pr(not-q), Pr(not-q/not-p) > Pr(not-q/p), Pr(not-q & not-p) > Pr(not-p)Pr(not-q); Pr(p/not-q) < Pr(p), Pr(not-q/p) < Pr(not-q), Pr(p & not-q) < Pr(p)Pr(not-q); Pr(q/not-p) < Pr(q), Pr(not-p/q) < Pr(not-p), Pr(q & not-p) < Pr(q)Pr(not-p).

5. D&M are negatively dependent; U&D are positively dependent; U&M are independent. Pr(D/M) = 0.04, Pr(U/D) = 0.36, Pr(U/M) = 0.30.

6. While the initial probabilities are a prima facie indication that smoking causes nose cancer, the second set of probabilities shows that location 'screens off' the cancer/smoking association, which suggests that smoking itself has no causal influence on cancer.

7. While the initial probabilities are a prima facie indication that the admissions process favours men, the second set of probabilities shows that within each faculty females turn out to be more successful than men. This suggests that faculty is influencing both gender of applicants and entrance success, and that the lower overall proportion of successful female applicants is due to their disproportionate representation in the more competitive Arts entrance competition, even though within both faculties the admissions process actually favours women. This is a case of Simpson's paradox.

Chapter 10

1. Example of (a): all men are mortal, Socrates is a man—so, Socrates is mortal. Example of (b): all men are bald, Meryl Streep is a man—so, Meryl Streep is bald. Example of (c): all women run fast, Usain Bolt is a woman—so, Usain Bolt runs fast.

   Since a valid argument is one where the truth of the premises guarantees the truth of the conclusion, a valid argument can't have true premises and a false conclusion.

2.

p	'not'-p	p-'or'-'not'-p
T	F	T
F	T	T

p	'not'-p	p-'and'-'not'-p	'not'-(p-'and'-'not'-p)
T	F	F	T
F	T	F	T

p	q	'not'-p	p-'and'-'not'-p	(p-'and'-'not'-p)-'→'-q
T	T	F	F	T
T	F	F	F	T
F	T	T	F	T
F	F	T	F	T

3. (a) false; (b) true; (c) true; (d) false. (The first two answers can be shown via truth tables, and the last two by attending to the proof rules for the relevant connectives.)

4. Let me illustrate just for Reductio Ad Absurdum ('Not' Introduction). The rule says: given p-'→'-q, p-'→'-not-q, move to 'not'-p. The table below shows that in all cases where the former statements are both true, the latter will be true too.

p	q	'not'-q	p-'→'-q	p-'→'-'not'-q	'not'-p
T	T	F	T	F	F
T	F	T	F	T	F
F	T	F	T	T	T
F	F	T	T	T	T

5. The truth table for '→' says that p-'→'-q is true as long as it's not the case that p is true and q is false. p $\vDash_{PROP}$ q means that q is semantically guaranteed to be true whenever p is, which semantically guarantees the truth of p-'→'-q— that is, $\vDash_{PROP}$ p → q. Conversely, if $\vDash_{PROP}$ p → q, it's semantically guaranteed not to be the case that p is true and q is false—that is, p $\vDash_{PROP}$ q.

INDEX

accidental properties 66, 80–2
analytic 45–8, 50, 52, 54
a posteriori 45–7, 50–2, 54
    necessities 59–60, 80–3
a priori 45–54, 58
    contingencies 59–61, 80–1
arithmetic 164–5, 167, 169–76
Aune, B. 56
axiom of comprehension 4,
    9–14
axiom of extensionality 4, 9, 13
Ayer, A. 58

base rate fallacy 110, 113
Bayes, T. 109
Bayes' Theorem 109–10, 113
Bayesianism 110
barber paradox 12–13
Bennett, J. 117
'bent' space 51–4
Berkeley, G. 48
Bigelow, J. 131
binary notation 32–3
Black, M. 84
Boolos, G. 163
Brown, J. 28

Cantor, G. 26, 35, 36
cardinality 30
causal theory of reference 76–8
causation 122–30
Cohen, P. 36
coherence, probabilistic 99, 101,
    107, 109
Colyvan, M. 28
completeness
    logical 149–53, 157, 158, 159, 161–2,
        168–9
    theoretical 166–9
conditional proof, rule of 144
conditionalization 107–10, 113
    Principle of 108–10
conditionals 110–12, 113–16
    counterfactual 115
    indicative 114–16
    material 111–12, 114, 140
    subjunctive 67, 114–16
confounding causes 125–30
contingency 45, 58–61, 66,
    67, 74
    a priori 59–61, 80
continuum hypothesis 35–6
    generalized 38–9

correlation 121–30
  spurious 125–9
credence 96

de dicto 79–80
de re 79–80, 82
degree of belief 96–101
denumerability 22–7, 31–2
Descartes, R. 48, 50
description theory of reference 76–7
diagonal argument 25–6, 35, 36, 37
domain of discourse 156, 162
Dummett, M. 163
Dutch Book Argument 98–9, 101,
  105, 107, 109

Edgington, D. 117
empiricism 48
essential properties 66–7, 80–2
Euclid 52, 55
  axioms of 52, 54–5, 165
  geometry 54, 164–5
Evans, G. 60

Fitting, M. 40
Frege, G. 14

geometry 48–54, 164, 165
  pure and applied 52–4
Gödel, K. 36, 157, 169–77
  numbering 170–4
  sentence 171–6
  theorem 169–76
Gowers, T. 56

Hacking, I. 102
Halbach, V. 148

Hayek, A. 102
Higgins, P. 28
Hitchcock, C. 131
Hodges, W. 148
Hofstadter, D. 177
Horwich, P. 117
Howson, C. 117
Hughes, C. 70
Hume, D. 48
Hunter, G. 163

idealization 97
identity of indiscernibles 84
incompleteness of second-order
  logic 161–2
indiscernibility of identicals 82, 84, 85
infinity 17–39

Jeffrey, R. 163
Julius (the inventor of the zip) 60–1,
  64, 74–5, 77, 79, 80, 81

Kahneman, D. 95, 102
Kant, I. 49
Kolomogorov, A. 90
  axioms of 89–92
Kripke, S. 59–60, 70, 76–7, 80, 85

Leibniz, G. 48
Lemmon, E. 148, 162
Lewis, D. 65, 70, 85, 105
Linda (the feminist bank teller) 95
Locke, J. 48
logic 137–62; see also completeness,
    logical consequence, metalogic,
    rules of inference, soundness
  modal 139

predicate 139, 153–9, 162, 165
propositional 139, 143–7
second-order 139, 159–62
theorem of 143, 156, 158
truth of 146, 157, 158–9, 168–9
logical consequence 142–6,
    149–57, 162
semantic xviii, 142, 144–6, 149–53,
    156–7, 158, 165
syntactic xviii, 142–5, 149–56,
    158, 165

Mackie, P. 85
Malinas, G. 131
Mellor, D. 102
meta-language 175
metalogic 138–9, 142
modality 67–8, 75, 79
modus ponens 144, 152–3
Moore, A. 40

Nagel, E. 177
natural selection 50
necessity 45, 58–63, 67–8, 72–3,
    78–83
a posteriori 59–60, 80–3
Newman, R. 177
non-denumerability 25–7, 31
numbers 17–39
integers 18, 23
irrational 19, 23–5
natural 17–18, 20–5, 167
rational 19, 23–4
real 19, 25–7, 31–6
numerals 17

object language 175

parallel postulate 52, 55
Peano, G. 164–5, 167
postulates of 165, 167, 169–70, 172,
    174–5
Pearl, J. 131
Penrose, R. 177
possibility 61–5, 67–9, 78–9, 81
natural 68–9
possible worlds 62–5, 68–9, 81
Potter, M. 15
power set 8–9
of the natural numbers 32–4
theorem 36–8
Principal Principle, the 105, 107
probabilities 89
conditional 91, 106–11
and frequencies 100
joint 91–4
objective 94, 99–100, 104–5, 121–2
personal 96
quantum 99–100
subjective 94–101, 104–5; see also
    credence, degree of belief
updating of 107–10
probabilistic dependence 120–2;
    see also correlation
probabilistic independence 119
proof 143, 145, 155
proper names 59, 74–8

quantifiers 139, 154–7
second-order 159–61
Quine, W. 56

randomized experiments 126–9
rationalism 48
recursive 159

recursively enumerable 159, 162
reductio ad absurdum 11, 144, 152
Reimer, M. 85
Rey, G. 56
rigid designation 75–6
Robertson, T. 85
rules of inference 143–4, 149–53,
    154–6, 161–2
Russell, Bertrand 11, 14
    paradox 11–14
    set 10–11
Russell, Bruce 56

Sainsbury, M. 85, 117
scope distinctions 73–4, 176
screening off 123–30
semantic tableaux xviii, 158
semantics 142, 151–3, 161–2,
    165–8
sets 3–39
    empty 5
    extensive notation for 3
    infinite 17–39
    intensive notation for 4
    intersection of 5
    naive theory of 4, 13–14
    membership of 4, 6–7
    power 8–9, 32–4, 36–8
    proper subsets 6, 20
    recursive 159
    recursively enumerable 159
    singleton 6
    subsets 6–9
    union of 5
Simpson's paradox 128, 130
Smith, P. 177
Smullyan, R. 40

soundness
    logical 149–53, 157, 158
    theoretical 166, 169–70, 172
Spinoza, B. 48
statistical fluctuations 129
Steinhart, E. 15, 28, 40
survey research 127–8
syntax 142, 151–3, 161–2, 165, 167–8
synthetic 45–54
synthetic a priori knowledge 47–54

Talbott, W. 117
theories, 3–4, 164–9
    axioms of, 165
    object 174
    meta- 174–6
    theorems of 165
    vocabulary of 164
Tiles, M. 15
truth-functional connectives
    139–41, 143–6, 154, 156–7
truth tables 140–1, 158
truth values 140–1, 145
Tversky, A. 95
type and token 19

undecidability of predicate
    logic 157–9
Urbach, P. 117
use and mention 18
utility 97
    expected 97

validity 137–8
Venn diagrams 90–4

Worrall, J. 131